One Dinner A Week, And Travels In The East

Charles Dickens

ONE DINNER A WEEK,

AND

TRAVELS IN THE EAST.

REPRINTED FROM

ALL THE YEAR ROUND,

CONDUCTED BY CHARLES DICKENS.

THE LONDON COTTAGE MISSION,

44, FINSBURY PAVEMENT, LONDON, E.C.

1884.

MR. WALTER AUSTIN.

Frontispie

ONE DINNER A WEEK.[*]

As my years, alas! are more than are
contained in half a century, I presume I
am considered to be in my second childhood when I find myself invited to attend
a children's party. I generally struggle to
accept these invitations, although I well may
feel suspicious of their covering a smile at
my protracted juvenility. Still, I am par-
tial to small people, and never like to miss
an opportunity of meeting them, and of learn-
ing something new about society in general,
which I usually find they are able to impart to me. But for the knowledge thus
acquired, I should never have discovered
that Jones, whom I esteemed as the most
pompous of old prigs, was so excellent a
help in making a dirt pudding, or that
Brown, whom I regarded as the prosiest
of bores, had so fanciful a talent for the
telling of a fairy-tale. Tomkins, too, I
thought a rather shallow fellow, till I
learned quite accidentally how profound
was his knowledge of the anatomy of
dolls, and how perfect was his skill in
setting fractured (wooden) legs, and mending broken (waxen) noses; while I must
candidly confess that my esteem for my
friend Robinson has enormously increased

[*] ALL THE YEAR ROUND, February 16, 1884.

since I have discovered how renowned he is for saddling a cockhorse, and how he distances all rivals in the art of making toffee.

Having thus a taste for juvenile festivities, I accepted with great pleasure a recent invitation by Mr. Walter Austin, of the London Cottage Mission, to come to one of his small weekly children's dinner-parties. Small, that is, in reference to the stature of the guests, but hardly to be called so in considering their numbers. The average attendance is upwards of five hundred, and, when funds enough are furnished by the charitable public, the pot is kept a boiling for as many as a thousand. "Small and early" is the rule of these little social gatherings, and though the hour named is noon, the guests are not so fashionable that they needs must be unpunctual. "First come, first served," is a motto fair to all, and one easily remembered by small boys with large appetites. So the cooks who are employed at 67, Salmon Lane, in the neighbourhood of Stepney, have no cause for complaint that their cookery is spoilt by waiting for late comers.

Salmon Lane has certainly an appetising sound, and seems not inappropriate as a place to give a dinner. On coming from a pantomime, one might expect, perhaps, to find it close to Cod's Head Court, and not far from Turtle Alley, or possibly Fried Sole Street. As I walked along the lane, which is somewhat of a long one, although it has no turning, I felt a trifle disappointed at not meeting some old friends, such as Mr. Chalks the milkman, and Mrs. Suds the laundress, with whom my panto-

WAITING AT THE DOOR.

Face page 4.

mime experience had long made me familiar. I confess I should have liked to see upon the shop-fronts such well - remembered names as, " Butcher, Mr. Shortweight," or "Baker, Mr. Crusty," and I should have further found reason for rejoicing come across a chimney-sweep whee perambulator, such as in the festive season I have seen upon the stage, or possibly a policeman being wheeled off in a wheel-barrow in the middle of a pelting shower of cabbages and carrots. Or if this delight was not to be, I might still have been content if I had but seen a row of water-rate collectors sitting in the stocks, or a kitchen-stuff supply-store, with the sign of the Hot Poker.

But the reality was not of this dramatic character. Salmon Lane, indeed, is a most prosaic thoroughfare, and when seen upon a foggy day, shows little to remind one of the glamour of the footlights. Its small houses are all of the most ordinary square-box, plain, back-slummy order of archi-tecture. Miles of similar dull, dreary, dismal, dirty little tenements surround it on all sides, and the eye of the æsthetic may look vainly for relief from the sad, wearisome monotony. To one who had been trudging through the slushy little streets, and courts, and alleys in the neighbourhood, the sight of the New Cottage Mission Hall, with its cheerful white brick frontage, and clean and well-kept aspect, was pleasant to the eye; and the mind rejoiced at the prospect of the pro-mised transformation-scene, wherein the good fairy Benevolence would defeat the

demon Hunger, who would be banished
from the blissful realms of steaming Irish
Stew !

The dining-room, or rather let me say
the banquet-hall, wherein on every Wednesday, from November until May, this
happy "change" takes place, which trans-
forms a crowd of wretched, hungry little
children into a cheerful-looking, happy
little company, is supplied with fourteen
tables, at each of which is fully room for
seating fourteen of the guests. Fifteen, or
even sixteen, sometimes manage to find
room, for a child of four or five, especially
when half-starved, can be put in a small
space. So the banquet-hall accommodates
above two hundred guests, and when these
have all been feasted they go chattering
away, and the next two hundred hungry
ones fill the vacant seats. In accordance with
a rule which is printed in clear type upon
the cards of invitation, or, to speak less
politely, upon the tickets for soup, each
guest comes provided with a plate—or
more commonly a basin, as being more
convenient for holding a big helping—and
likewise with a spoon, of very varying
dimensions, and in few cases propor-
tionate to the mouth it has to feed.
Many of the bigger children had, I noticed,
nothing better than a battered teaspoon,
while one remarkably small guest, who
might have sat for Tiny Tim, had the
forethought to be furnished with a weapon
so prodigious, that he seemed prepared for
supper with that illustrious host, in connection with whom there is a proverb about
a long spoon.

THE RUSH FOR DINNER. *Face page* 6.

On the morning of my visit the hall was
three times filled, and the order of pro-
cedure was the same in every case. First
entered the guests, marching in quick time
to music of their own making, a chattering chorus in the minor, with brisk
pedal accompaniment. Attendants quickly
followed, bearing two enormous tin tureens
of Irish stew, one to each end of the room.
Then a whistle sounded shrilly, and silence
was proclaimed, and to the tune of the
Old Hundredth the children rose and sang
a short and simple grace, whereof the final
line bore reference to "feasting in Paradise," which must seem a heavenly pleasure
to a hungry little child.

Young singers, as a rule, are apt to drag
the time, but I am bound to say the fault
was here by no means to be found. Indeed,
a critic might have fancied that the grace
towards its close was just a trifle hurried,
and certainly the "Amen" was sung with
an alacrity which showed no sign of drag-
ging. Very possibly, however, this was
due, not quite so much to the musical
instruction which the singers had received,
as to the toothsome and delightful savour
of the stew. This with a delicious fragrance
floated in the air, and set the mouth
watering with pleasant expectation, so that
it was small wonder that the time was
never dragged.

Then there arose a hungry clamour,
which was speedily subdued, for when
once the little tongues had tasted of the
stew, they ceased with one consent to
waste their energy in prattling. And
although I saw no sign of unfair striving of

the stronger to get helped before the weakly, there was certainly a great out-stretching of the arms and uprising of the hands, which, but for the fact of their holding plates and basins, might have called to mind the Crowd Scene in the German Julius Cæsar. Hands and arms, however, had soon other work to do, for plates and basins were filled speedily, and handed to their owners. Unlike most public dinners, there was no cause to complain here of the sluggishness of waiters. Miss Napton, the kind lady who presides over the feasts, and the young ladies who come every Wednesday to help her, are, by constant practice, deft and active with their work, and give general satisfaction to the host and to the guests. If in her capacity of waitress any of them wished to apply for a new place, there would be no question of her getting a good character. One of these lady helps, if I may venture so to call them, is a lady by her title as well as by her courtesy and gentle birth and bearing. All gratitude and honour be to lady helps like Lady Colin Campbell and Miss Gordon, who never stint their service. And it is surely a good work to bring to the East End the gracious manners of the West, and lend a kindly hand to bridge the social chasms which are said by some to yawn between the rich and the poor, but which are not so deep but that good nature can soon fathom them with the helping of good sense.

But let us return to our mutton, or, rather, to our Irish stew, whereof, according to the cookery-books, mutton ought to

Face page 8.

LADY COLIN CAMPBELL SERVING THE IRISH STEW.

be the meat. But of the stew in Salmon
Lane the principal ingredient is that
"giant-like ox-beef" which has played such
havoc with the house of Fairy Mustard-
seed. Beef is here preferred, as being,
perhaps, stronger in its potency to nourish
and give power to small elbows and plump-
ness to pinched cheeks. Good, savoury,
substantial, wholesome, toothsome, and
nutritious, I certainly can certify I found
this children's food; a mess sufficing both
for meat and drink, of beef, and rice, and
vegetables, well-blended and well-boiled,
with nothing tough or stringy to harass
mastication, and with a dash of curry-
powder to help it to digest. Since six the
previous morning the cauldron had been
simmering, and the cooks hard at their
work, and the result was really quite a
triumph of their industry and art.

"Mak' yourself at whoam, sir, an' tak'
girt mouthfuls!" said a cheery farmer to
me, when, after walking through his
turnips, I found sufficient appetite to join
him in his onslaught on a half-boiled leg
of pork. I called to mind his kind advice
as I looked along the tables, and saw the
wistful eyes that watched the helping of
the meat. I thought that if "girt mouthfuls" were the rule with these small
feeders, the chances of a choking fit could
hardly be remote. But to take great
mouthfuls is not easy with a teaspoon, and
this in very many cases was the implement
employed. My notions of self-help, especially at dinner, might astonish Dr. Smiles,
but if I were very hungry, and were allowed
to help myself to Irish stew, I should not

select a teaspoon as my weapon for the occasion.

The picture of little Oliver asking for more, and thereby astounding the awful Mr. Bumble, could never find a parallel at these poor little children's dinner-parties. There is nothing of the Bumble about good Mr. Austin, and any little hungry, half-starved Olivers, or Olivias, or Jims, or Jacks, or Jills, may have their plates refilled as often as they please. Miss Jill may eat her fill, with no scruple and no stint, and Master Jack may peg away until he is "serenely full," like the salad-eating epicure described by Sydney Smith, and has the pleasant sensation, immortalised by Leech, of feeling as though his jacket were buttoned. This, with most of the Jacks present on the morning of my visit, would have been a new sensation, and one difficult to realise, for buttons seemed a luxury whereof not many could boast. A pin or piece of string was mostly used by way of substitute, though at the throat of one young masher sparkled such metallic lustre that I fancied he wore studs. But on a closer view I found that the brilliant was a bit of wire, which probably had once adorned a soda-water bottle. This served to keep his coat, which was three sizes too big for him, from falling off his shoulders, and making known the fact that there was nothing under it to cover his bare skin.

It may be. guessed from the last paragraph that, as concerns their dinner costume, Mr. Austin is by no means too exacting with his guests. White chokers

A QUIET CORNER.   *Face page* 10.

and dress-coats are far from being neces-
sary, and it is not esteemed essential
that all trousers should be black. The
nearest approach that I could find to a
dress-coat was a garment which had been
denuded of its tails and shortened for a
jacket. Of ties there were none, neither
white, nor black, nor grey, though in some
cases their place was supplied by a thin,
threadbare strip of shoddy worsted, called,
in mockery, a "comforter," which dangled
to the waist, and if it afforded little comfort
to the wearer, it appeared to be of service
as a napkin and a handkerchief. Masher
cuffs and cut-throat collars were conspicuous by their absence, and only in one
instance was a shirt-front to be seen, and
this was simply from the fact that the
young swell who displayed it wore neither
coat nor vest.

The girls were just a shade less shabby
than the boys; for a shawl, though thin,
may cover a multitude of sins in the
raiment underneath it, and a bit of faded
ribbon or a fragment of a feather may
serve to give some colour to a sorely battered bonnet or a sadly frayed-out dress.
One pretty child I noticed who seemed
better clad than most, and looked quite a
little lady as she sat at table, the scarlet
poppies in her hat adding colour to the
paler roses on her cheek. But, alas! the
hat was only lent for the occasion, and
when she left her seat to tell me her sad
tale—how she had had no meat since
Wednesday, and scarce enough bread
since, and there were three children at
home, and no father to feed them, and

mother out of work—as she stood to
tell me this, I called to mind the saying
about "desinit in piscem" which I had
learned at school, for although "formosa
superne" with the poppies in her hat, the
poor little woman boasted the fishiest ot
boots.

Other cases I could cite of singularity
in costume, which might have appeared
humorous if they had not been so pathetic.
Perhaps the funniest of all, and also
possibly the saddest, were a couple of
small people who toddled in together, and
when seated seemed inseparable, like the
famous Siam twins. The cause of this
close union was, I found, an oilskin table-
cloth, which, as the day was wet and
stormy, had been lent them for a cloak.

I hope that no reader will fancy from
the manner of my writing that I have any
thought of making silly, ill-timed fun of
these poor hungry little folks, or of amusing
myself by raising a coarse laugh at their
expense. God help them! I would
sooner throw my pen into the fire
and never write another word that
should appear in print. I am not a
man of sentiment, or much inclined to
snivel at the sight of a dead donkey or a
babe crying for the moon. But, albeit
unused to the melting mood, my eyes were
somewhat moistened by looking at these
little ones, and as I talked with them and
cheered them as well as I was able, if I
had not done my best to laugh—not at
them, mind, but with them—I think I
must have cried. A child without a plaything is a pitiable being, and here were

ONE SPOON FOR TWO.   *Face page* 12.

children by the dozen not merely without playthings, but without the hope of play. Most of them had to work, and to work hard for a living, and probably not one in ten had ever learned to play. One urchin told me, with some pride, that he could weekly add some six or seven shillings to the family support by working every day about ten hours at a stretch. To fix the bristles in a scrub-brush is a slow way to grow rich, for you only gain a penny if you fill two hundred holes, and you will soon find that your fingers suffer from the work. Nor is making match-boxes a lucrative employment when you are paid twopence a gross for them, providing your own paste. These were two out of a score of handicrafts, described to me, which just save from starvation many children in the East. Poor little ill-paid toilers ! I might have well been moved to tears as I listened to their sad tales and looked at their pale cheeks. But I liked better to see them brighten with the sunshine of a smile, and so I tried to cheer them and not grieve at their sad plight.

As to the good done by these dinners there can be little doubt. They would be well worth the giving, were it only for the fact of their affording to the guests one bright half-hour of happiness to think of and look forward to through all the dull, dark week. But their physical well-doing is far more deeply felt. One good dinner a week may save a child from starving, and be the means, if it be sickly, of helping it to health. That the parents in the neighbourhood, as well as the poor children,

quite appreciate the value of the stew
of Salmon Lane is well proved by the
many applications which are made for
leave to come and eat of it. Here is just
one specimen, picked at random from a
heap, and copied literatim. There can be
surely no mistake about the force of the
appeal, although the writer might perhaps
have improved the spelling somewhat had
he conceived the notion that it would be
seen in print :

"Gentelman i should feel Abligh to you
if you would give me a fue tickets has
my Wife has gorn to the Infirney at
Bromly and Left me With 5 Children has
i ham out of Work and no wan to support
them I should feall gratley Abligh John
McIntier 31 Brenton st."

In reply to sundry questions touching
management and maintenance, Mr. Austin
kindly gave me an account of his steward-
ship, that is, his Irish stew-ardship. He
first started on his mission—to help the
East End poor—more than a dozen years
ago ; but the first of his small dinners was
given on the first Wednesday in 1879,
which, it chanced, was New Year's Day.
Since then he has issued his invitations
weekly, except on one occasion, throughout
the winter months and far into the spring.
The one sad exception happened in the
January of last year. On this terrible
Black Wednesday, the poor little folk who
came to feast as usual were sent empty
away. Due notice had been given that
through lack of funds that day no dinner
could be had ; but the guests came notwithstanding, for hunger often leads to

PACKING UP.   *Face page* 14.

hoping against hope, and it was a hard task to persuade them of the melancholy truth.

Considering its excellence, the expense of the banquet can be hardly thought extravagant ; for the dinner-bill is barely more than fourpence-farthing for each one of the guests. So that, in fact, to save a child from starving, and give him a good feed, scarce exceeds the cost of swallowing an oyster, as the market price now rules. Perhaps the sybarite who sucks down half-a-score by way of prelude to his dinner may, in some visit of the nightmare, after extra heavy feasting, be haunted by the ghosts of those half-dozen hungry children whom his oysters might have fed. As penance for his gluttony, he may enjoy the novel luxury of doing a good deed, by sending Mr. Austin a donation for his dinners ; and, by way of wholesome exercise, he may try a course of East End district-visiting, which he will find vastly different to the visiting in the West.

To support the Cottage Mission, the dinner-bills included, Mr. Austin receives yearly about seventeen hundred pounds. Gifts from voluntary donors are all he has to help him ; and the more money they give the more food will be given, the more visits be paid, and the more good will be done. The expenses of the management are most carefully restricted to the lowest point consistent with the work being well-done. Funds are not wasted on fine buildings, or on ornamental gentlemen, who receive a princely salary for doing poorish work. Any one who sends a sovereign to be spent upon the stew, may be sure he will thereby be filling fifty little mouths, and that fifty little bodies will be gladdened by his gift. And there is no fear of the benefit being ill-bestowed. The district-visitors who help the kindly host in his good work will scruple not to penetrate the slummiest of the slums, and will invite to dinner only those in direst need.

The Cottage Mission work, as carried on by Mr. Austin, is completely unsectarian, and by neither church nor chapel can a fair reason be assigned for holding aloof from its support. When he meets with a sad case of spiritual destitution—and such cases are just now not uncommon in the East—it is by simple Gospel teaching that he strives for its relief; and when, as on these winter Wednesdays, he does his best to succour cases of bodily distress, a hungry little child need learn no "Open Sesame" in order to gain entrance to his hospitable hall. That he is doing a good work I am most thoroughly persuaded, or I certainly should never send this paper to the press. They who may be moved by it to help him in his mission need merely sign their names at the bottom of a cheque, and post it to his office, at Number Forty-four in Finsbury Pavement, where their autographs will be most thankfully received.

TRAVELS IN THE EAST.

A SERIES OF ARTICLES

REPRINTED FROM

ALL THE YEAR ROUND,

CONDUCTED BY CHARLES DICKENS.

TRAVELS IN THE EAST.

PART I.*

BOOKS of Eastern travel have been plentiful enough, and many are the marvels which have therein been recorded. Volumes varying in their size as well as in their style have been as thick as autumn leaves that strew the brooks of Vallombrosa; which, a recent tourist states, is nowadays by no means so remarkable for leafiness as in Milton's time it may have been. Facts and fiction have been copiously mingled in these records, and they who may have smiled at the fables of Herodotus may have likewise been amused by the fancies of Eothen. From St. Paul to Captain Burnaby is rather a long step, but each of them has given some account of Eastern travelling, and writers who have helped to fill the gap between them have, in their turn, done something to enlighten Western ignorance of Oriental sights, and scenery, and life, and locomotion.

So that when I first thought of putting into print some record of my recent travels in the East, I confess I felt alarmed lest I might quite inadvertently be found committing plagiary. Yet a second thought

* ALL THE YEAR ROUND, March 1, 1884.

convinced me that my fears were
wholly groundless. For the fact is, I have
never travelled farther East than Venice,
and I have no thought of attempting to
rival Mr. Ruskin, and to write about that
city. The isles of Greece are only known
to me in Byron, and, except in picture-
galleries, I have never seen the Parthenon.
Home-lover as I am, I have never gone to
Egypt, much less to Jerusalem, whereof,
apart from sacred lore, the only things I
know are its artichokes and ponies.

But the country I have visited in my
late travels in the East may be reached with
no long flight by a home-bird such as I
am. The strange scenes I have looked at
lie no farther off than Stepney, and the
most distant point I gained must certainly
be placed within three miles of London
Bridge, and may readily be reached by
road, or rail, or river. In fact, the purpose
of my journey was to make myself acquainted, in some degree at least, with the
poor at the East End, and to gain a certain
knowledge of their dwellings and their
doings.

Being wholly new to the strange land
I wished to see, I thought it prudent at
the outset to engage a skilful guide, who
should direct my progress. The conductor
whom I had the good fortune to select
was Mr. Walter Austin, who for years has
been the manager of the London Cottage
Mission. This gentleman has long been
familiar with the country and the customs
of its people, and, although as yet not
famous in the Annals of the Geographical
Society, he has certainly done wonders in

the way of Eastern exploration. Some account of his good work there has been published in these pages,* and having seen how well he was able to conduct himself on the occasion there described, I felt sure of a safe guide if he would personally conduct me in my course of Eastern travel.

Explorers who intend to visit a strange country provide themselves in general with a vast number of things which may be useful in emergencies, that somehow never happen, and so, when starting on my journey—on the morning, let me add, of the first Wednesday in February—I thought it only prudent to carry an umbrella, which, except a sandwich, was indeed my only baggage. I might have foreseen that the precaution would be quite needless, and, in fact, throughout the day it never rained a drop. Even the City streets were clean as I pushed my way along them from the station miscalled "Mansion House," the station being in Cannon Street, while the Mansion House is not. So on reaching Aldgate Pump, which, if memory serves me rightly, once was famous in a farce, I decided to take neither a hansom nor a tram, but to walk, like Mr. Weston and such heroes of the footpath, along the couple of miles or so which led to Salmon Lane.

There I arrived at noon, and found the usual little crowd of Wednesday diners-out. All had their spoons and plates, and doubtless, too, their appetites, quite ready for the feast which was about to put some

---

* ALL THE YEAR ROUND, New Series, Vol. 33, p. 299, "One Dinner a Week."

colour into their pale cheeks. Above a
hundred entered while I stood at the door,
and though I kept a sharp look-out, I
declare I only noticed one good pair of
boots. Three tiny little trots had scarce a
pair of soles between them, and many a
Baby Barefoot might have been observed.
One little Cinderella came in a fancy
costume, which looked as though it had
been made of an old counterpane of patch-
work, and I wished that some good fairy
could have seen her wretched slippers,
which were certainly transparent, though
they were not made of glass. Then possibly the fairy might have waved her magic
wand and have presented the poor child
with a good strong pair of shoes. Ah,
ladies of the West, who have children of
your own, whom you delight to see well
clad, will you sometimes spare a thought
for these poor children of the East?
When you think Miss Lucy's cloak is
beginning to look shabby, or that Master
Tommy's jacket is just a bit too small for
him, or his boots a trifle tight—for he is
such a growing boy, and his appetite so
hearty, bless him!—will you kindly make
a parcel of the raiment you discard and
send it to the Cottage Mission Hall in
Salmon Lane? Thus, at no great cost or
trouble, you may assume the part of the
benevolent good fairy, and by your per-
formance for their benefit, confer much
real comfort on many a little Jack and
Jill, and Sue, and Cinderella, who are now
so poorly clothed.

My guide was ready for a start, soon
after his small guests had sung their usual

Face page 22.

grace. We left the lady-helpers all busy
at their work, and enveloped in a cloud of
incense as it were to the deity of dining,
arising from the big tureens of fragrant,
steaming stew. Alas! our nostrils had
been filled with odours far less savoury
when, after three hours' travelling, we
next entered the hall. There was, however, a faint smell of something like to
cookery in the first house that we visited;
faint, that is, when compared with the fine
savour we had sniffed while the stew was
being served. Still, the smell was quite as
strong as one could well expect, when one
had traced it to its source, and found that
it proceeded from so very small a pot.
This was slowly simmering on a fire which
for its smallness must have been made to
match. Despite its littleness, however,
it made a bright spot in the room, which
otherwise was sadly dull and dismal to the
eye, and brought to mind a vision of the
blue chamber in Blue Beard, for the walls
were of that colour, excepting in the places
where the plaster had peeled off. There
was no cloth on the table and no carpet
on the floor, and but a scanty show of
crockery on the shelf. Signs of comfort
there were none, though there was certainly
a cat, whose presence often seems to give
a room a cosy look. But pussy in this case
looked sorely thin and careworn, as though
mice were rather scarce. Near the ceiling,
which was less than eight feet from the
floor, there hung a poor little canary,
imprisoned in a cage so small that it could
hardly hop. As, during my whole visit,
he stood silent on his perch, and neither

sang nor even chirped a single note, perhaps the inference is fair that his life was
not more cheerful than that of the cat—
not to mention the six other usual inmates
of the room.

Curiosity is vulgar and may be offensive;
but I could not help confessing that I felt
a little curious as to what was in the pot.
" Three penn'orth of meat, penn'orth of
potatoes, ha'porth of pot-herbs, and a pinch
or so of salt." That was in the pot with
about a quart of water; and that was the
dinner for mother and two children—Joey,
a small boy of twelve, and Jim, a biggish
one of four; her other two to-day being
guests in Salmon Lane. Mother is a
comely, bright-eyed, civil-speaking woman,
"forty-two last birthday," she says without
reluctance, and hardly smiles when told
that she looks younger than her age. Fifth
of November is her birthday, remembers
it by Guy Fawkes. Father's forty-eight.
Gone to the hospital he is, because he's
got hurt in the back. His birthday was
yesterday. Oh no, sir, 'tweren't like that.
Father didn't have no birthday jollifica-
tion. Bless you, he's too poor to spend
his money in a spree. You see, he's a
dock-labourer, and, now work is short,
there's such a crowding at the gates.
That's how he got jammed. A strongish
man he is, too, but not being overfed, you
see, a small hurt tells on him. Wages?
Well, he earns two-and-elevenpence a day,
when he can get full work, but there isn't
one day out of three he gets it. Yes, I
know there's many as works half-time
'cause they likes to. But he's not one to

"Three pennorth o' meat, pennorth o' potatoes and a pinch o salt."

Face page 24.

shirk or laze about in that way. There ain't a drop of idle blood in all his body, that there ain't.

Mother looks a little fierce as she says this, and her bright eyes gleam defiance of attack upon the absent. I divert her wrath by pointing to the sad want of repair which is apparent in the premises, and her anger blazes out at the mean greed of the landlord, whom she holds to blame.

"He won't do nothing, bless you; not spend a penny, he won't. Yes, the plaster's off the walls, and the floor is half in holes, and the roof it lets the rain in. But it's no good our complaining. House-room's precious scarce, although you wouldn't think it to see the miles there is of 'em. Four shillings a week we pay for our two rooms [which, except a staircase, is all the house contains], and if we were to leave he'd easy find another tenant."

Might we see where they slept? Why, yes, we might, and welcome. Mother briskly leads the way upstairs, and I, as briskly following, get a blow from a low beam, which sets my brain reflecting that a sudden rise in life is not unfraught with danger. The bed-chamber, we find, is of the same size as the sitting-room—or, shall I say, the parlour? for there were not many chairs in it—the floor, say, ten feet square, with seven feet to the ceiling. There are a couple of beds, both covered with coarse sackcloth, and neither showing sign of either sheet or blanket. The parents sleep in one and their four children in the other; and for the purposes of toilet there is an old cracked looking-glass. The floor is bare, the walls are blue, the ceiling rain-discoloured; there is neither chair, nor table, nor clothes-closet, nor washing-stand. I presume there is a pump somewhere handy in the neighbourhood, but, as far as I can see, there is nothing in the house to serve the purpose of ablution.

Returning to the parlour — or, shall I say, the kitchen? — I remark upon the damp which stains the corner by the cupboard. The last tenant, it seems, had used this closet as a dog-kennel, and had left it rather disagreeably over-populated and sorely needing disinfection. Assuming for the nonce the part of sanitary inspector, I go behind the house, and there I find a small enclosure, wherein, if one may judge from the filth which lies a-festering, any rubbish may be shot, and no count be taken of the shooting. A heap of this lay piled against the wall whose dampness I had noticed, and I proclaim my opinion that the vestry ought to see to it. "They won't do nothing," says mother; "not if you goes on your knees to 'em. Why, yes, it do smell bad at times, but there, it's no use our complaining. The landlord 'ud soon turn us out if he caught us a-grumbling. How long has it been wet? Well, mostly since last winter. Ah yes, Mr. Austin, when I think how those three children were all took away so sudden, one after another, somehow it's my belief the dampness might ha' done it. Yes, sir, they all died in a fortnight; leastways, in fifteen days they did. Oh no, sir, they wasn't the last tenant's [for she had told the tale so calmly that I put the question]. My own children they was, now weren't they, Mr. Austin? An' they all died last April. An' a jolly good cry I had when they was took. An' I've had many a cry since. But there, crying ain't no good. Poor little souls, maybe they're happy now they're dead, an' whiles they lived I know they hadn't much to make 'em happy."

While she is telling me this tragedy, I see that mother's bright eyes look a little dim, and there is a something in her voice which is like a smothered sob. But I can detect no other sign of sorrow. I indeed might fancy that she hardly felt her recent loss. However, I know better, from having in my life had some acquaintance with poor people. Any one who knows them knows how great is their endurance of the arrows of affliction, and how little they indulge in the luxury of grief. "I wouldn't wish him back, though," added a poor mother, after telling me how fever had just killed her only boy. "He's better where he is, I'm pretty sure of that, sir; and though I were main proud of him, I wouldn't wish him back."

The first halt in my travelling had been in a Court, and the next was in a Place. There was nothing very courtly in the court, or princely in the place—although they both alike bore the title of the Regent, whose memory be blest. The scene of court-life I had witnessed prepared me for one similar; but I found one poorer still.

In this royally-named quarter all the houses look alike—small square boxes of bad brickwork, a score of feet or so in height, with one room on the first floor—

there seldom is a second—and one room
on the ground. In the brick-box we next
visited there lived in the ground room a
widow with her family, and she for one-
and-ninepence weekly let the top room to
another widow and her family, on whom
we came to call. But it is not quite so
easy to make calls in the East as it is in
the West. When the mistress is away, it
often happens there is nobody to answer at
the door. This was so when we arrived,
and we were puzzled for admittance as
there was neither bell, nor knocker, nor
handle to the door. Presently, however,
there came a little child who had been
dining at the Hall, and she speedily produced the handle from its hiding-place,
and gave us entrance to her home. Here
was no cat, no canary, no gleam of feeble
firelight to enliven the sad gloom. The
bed had not been made, there was indeed
no bed to make. It is true there was a
bedstead and some bits of sacking on it, all
huddled in a heap; but to have "made"
it into a bed would have puzzled any house-
maid who wished to do the work. Two chairs,
a small deal table, and a sack half-filled
with straw, were the only other furniture,
except a broken fender; and this seemed a
real luxury, for had there been a fire, it
could have proved of little use. A big
bundle of new sailcloth lay on the small
table, which was further occupied by a
hank or two of rope-yarn; so that its
service as a work-table, much more than
as a dinner-table, was, by these encum-
brances, made present to the mind. Grandmother and mother were employed in

making hammocks. Stiffish work it seemed, too, for the cloth was hard to sew. They could earn four-and-sixpence by making half-a-score, which was as much as ever one could manage in a week. The worst of it was that they lost much precious time in walking to the workshop, where they drilled the eyelet-holes, which they could not do at home.

The little girl had hastened home to get on with her "splicings." These she made with the tarred yarn, whereof her fingers bore the trace. A toughish job it was, for hands so thin and weak. Making twenty pairs for sixpence, she could earn three shillings a week. But did she never go to school? Oh yes; she had been pretty regular since Christmas, till just now. Mother thought it mightn't matter if she kept away a bit, now work was coming in, for it had been so very slack. Home-work or school-work, which did she prefer? for it appeared that the poor child had seldom any chance of the alternative of play. Oh, she liked home-work the best, she answered rather quickly, as though there could not be a doubt. But surely it was harder? Oh yes; it certainly was harder, but then it brought in something, and mother was so poor.

A pleasant, civil-speaking, pretty, sad-eyed little maiden she appeared as she stood by me, enlightening my ignorance of the commerce of the East. Thirteen on her next birthday, although seeing her small limbs I should have guessed her two years less. There was a shy smile on her lips as she corrected my mistake in sup-

posing that she had to sleep somewhere on
the floor. Oh no; grandmother and
mother, they both slept on the bed, and
she slept at their feet, and there were
the three children, and they lay on the
floor. Yes, they all three slept together on
the sack down in the corner there, between
the bedstead and the wall. Clearly the
little woman hardly thought herself a
child; she probably was nursemaid, if not
housekeeper and cook. Clearly, too, the
children had not grown very big, for the
sack whereon they slept was barely a yard
wide. But, I could not help reflecting, six
to sleep in that small room, and two of the
six certainly, if not three nearly, adults!
Perhaps for sake of warmth overcrowding
might be pardoned, if it were not hurtful
to health. But here the bedroom was a
workshop, and the little air there was in it
must have well-nigh been exhausted before
the day was done. Still, there were six to
sleep in it, and but one bed for three of
them, and for the other three a sack. And
had they nothing for a covering? "Oh yes,
sir," the little girl replied, "we have our
clothes." Clothes! Poor little child! Were a
bitter frost to come, her clothes would hardly
give much comfort. All she wore was a
thin jacket pinned together at the throat,
and a scanty skirt beneath, and a crippled
pair of boots; and, as far as could be seen,
a pair of cotton socks were all the linen
she possessed.

Had she ever had a doll? or tasted a
plum-pudding? or gathered a wild prim-
rose? or been taken to a pantomime?
Many a query like to these I felt inclined

to ask of this hard-working little maiden, who had answered very prettily in a soft and gentle voice the many questions I had put. But there were her splicings to be done, and we were taking up her time, and she could ill-afford to waste the only money she possessed. To make up for the precious minutes she had lost in telling us her story, I slipped something in her hand while bidding her good-bye ; and from the stare which it attracted, and the smile which quickly followed, I came to the conclusion that a coin not made of copper is not a common gift to a poor child in the East.

Here for the present I must pause, for I have filled the space assigned to me. They who would hear further of what happened in my course of Eastern travel will do me the favour to wait until next week.

TRAVELS IN THE EAST.

PART II.*

A CARAVAN is not uncommon in the East, and when a traveller falls in with one, he generally visits it. I should have as little dreamed of finding a cream ice in the desért as a caravan in Stepney; but somehow I fell in with one, and found it well worth visiting. As it was hidden in a sort of oasis as it were, a traveller might easily have passed, and not caught sight of it. But the sharp eyes of my guide were not to be deceived, and a single glance enabled him to indicate its whereabouts.

The oasis wherein the caravan had halted was not far from the spot I have described in my last paper. Although by way of euphemy I call it an oasis, it bore no trace of verdure or refreshing vegetation; and in fact it differed little in its dark and dismal ugliness from the dull and dreary district that surrounded it. Perhaps 'it might appear that I was using a misnomer if I were to speak of this same region as a desert, for in the space of three miles square there live above a million people. I simply speak of an oasis, because I am

* ALL THE YEAR ROUND, March, 8, 1884.

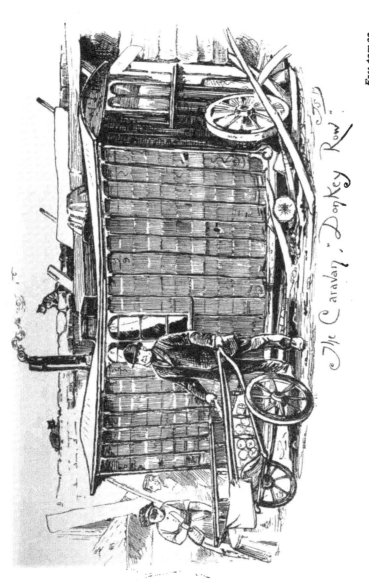

The Caravan, "Donkey Row"

Face page 32.

describing my late travels in the East, and
I may as well endeavour to impart some
Oriental flavour to my narrative. In the
directory, however, my oasis is more prosily
put down as " King's Arms Yard," abutting
upon Carr Street. After quitting Regent's
Place, it seemed a fit advancement to be
brought to King's Arms Yard, and as far
as the name went, one could hardly think
it strange to find a caravan in Carr Street.
This thoroughfare, however, like certain
lordly folk, is honoured with a second title ;
which, although distinguishing, has not yet
been inserted in the postal directory. The
dwellers in the neighbourhood have styled
it " Donkey Row," possibly because of the
preponderance of costermongers, who mostly
keep their carriages, among its influential
residents.

After a glance at this last paragraph, the
intelligent reader will have readily sur-
mised that the caravan I saw was a yellow,
old, roofed vehicle, which had probably
belonged to a showman or a gipsy. Doubtless it had journeyed many a mile in shady
lanes, and over sunny heaths, and breezy
open commons ; and had halted in the
shelter of many a leafy wood, ere it came
to its last resting-place in this great wilderness of brick. But its wanderings were
over now. Its rural haunts and hiding-
places would see its yellow face no more.
Its wheels had been removed—and sold by
the last occupant—it had come down in the
world, and had sunk helpless on the ground,
and having ceased to be a vehicle, was now
hired as a house, at a shilling a week rental,
by a reputable tenant.

This house, or caravanserai as Oriental-
ists might call it, not being very capacious,
could only hold one room, and this room,
though not very large, yet served as cellar,
kitchen, scullery, dining-room, and draw-
ing-room, workshop, library, and bedroom
for a couple of old people. Opposite the
doorway, which was half closed by a hatch,
there was a bed at the far end, which
filled the space from side to side—if the
word "far" may be used to denote so
small a distance. Between the doorway
and the bed—in the dining-room, that is—
there were a work-table, or rather a work-
bench, and a chair, and in the corner to
the left there stood a little iron stove, with
a smoke-pipe through the roof, which barely
served to let the smoke out. A small old
man stood by the table tying up in little
bundles the firewood he had cut. The
house being such a tiny one, its contents
were small to match, and the bundles were
so little that they seemed to be intended
for especially small fires. It might easily
be guessed, too, that the little old man was
making them for a woefully small price.

Above the bed, that is about three feet
from the floor, there was a narrow little
shelf, which held a little crockery and some
few little odds and ends, which seemed
somehow to impart the notion to my mind
that a petticoat was somewhat familiar to
the place. Among them was a little bottle,
holding a little water and a little sprig of
fir; which, being carefully preserved, had
possibly been gathered from a last year's
Christmas-tree. Beside it stood a little flower-
pot with a couple of green hyacinths, green,

"1/6? a hundred as sure as my name's Jonas"

Face page 24.

but giving show of coming richly-coloured bloom. These latter were the gift of some Good lady Samaritan who had visited the little house, and thought a little floral decoration would improve it as a dwelling. "She gives me a little treat like," remarked the old man gratefully; "an' it makes a man feel cheerful to see a bit o' green about him while he's working."

It seemed well that there was something pleasant in the place, for the look outside was certainly not cheering. The yard lay inches deep in dirt, so that the notice appeared needless that there was no thoroughfare. All around him looked indeed in a slovenly condition, albeit the old man declared he got on "pretty tidily." He would confess, however, that his dwelling was a trifle draughty in cold weather. Draughty certainly it must have been, not to say even tempestuous, when the stormy winds did blow; and not very warm either when Jack Frost was at the door, and there was only half an inch or so of deal to stop his entrance. The caravan required caulking as badly as an old boat. There were great cracks between the boards, which seemed to make the walls transparent, and certainly the inmates could not truthfully complain of any want of ventilation.

Half sheltered by a shed, just in front of his own doorway, a couple of sons of the old man were, like him, busy cutting firewood. With a gusty drizzle falling, and the ground so deep in slush, the yard appeared a dampish place for such an occupation. When questioned as to income, the old man showed no reticence. He frankly stated that he made four hundred or so bundles in a week, and sold them, being small, at eighteenpence the hundred. But he had to go about with a barrow for the sale of them, and the hiring of that vehicle reduced the weekly profits. Still, he and his old lady somehow managed to live on, and they were both of the same age, which might seem a little singular, and, being matched in years, they might last it out together. Seventy-six they were, and that was the real truth, as surely and as certainly as that his name was Jonas. And he was born in Willow Gardens, nigh to Curtain Road. Ah, 'twere a'most in the country then. Well, yes, now you came to think of it, the name did sound a pretty one, and seemed a little rural like. Yes, they got on fairish well, except of a hard winter. But times were fairish bad, too, seeing as they really hadn't bought a pound of butchers'-meat this two years. "Indeed," added the old man, "I do believe we'd a'most forgotten how it tasted like, till we got that Christmas-dinner as you gave us, Mr. Austin."

The old wood-cutter put forth his right hand as he said this, and gave my guide a hearty grip of gratitude, which showed how well the Christmas-meal still lingered in his memory. While taking leave of him I saw that there was pasted by the doorway a legal-looking document, which proved to be a notice of distress for rent. It was dated the 3rd of August in last year, and was addressed in clerkly hand to Mr. William Glibbery—not a bad name for

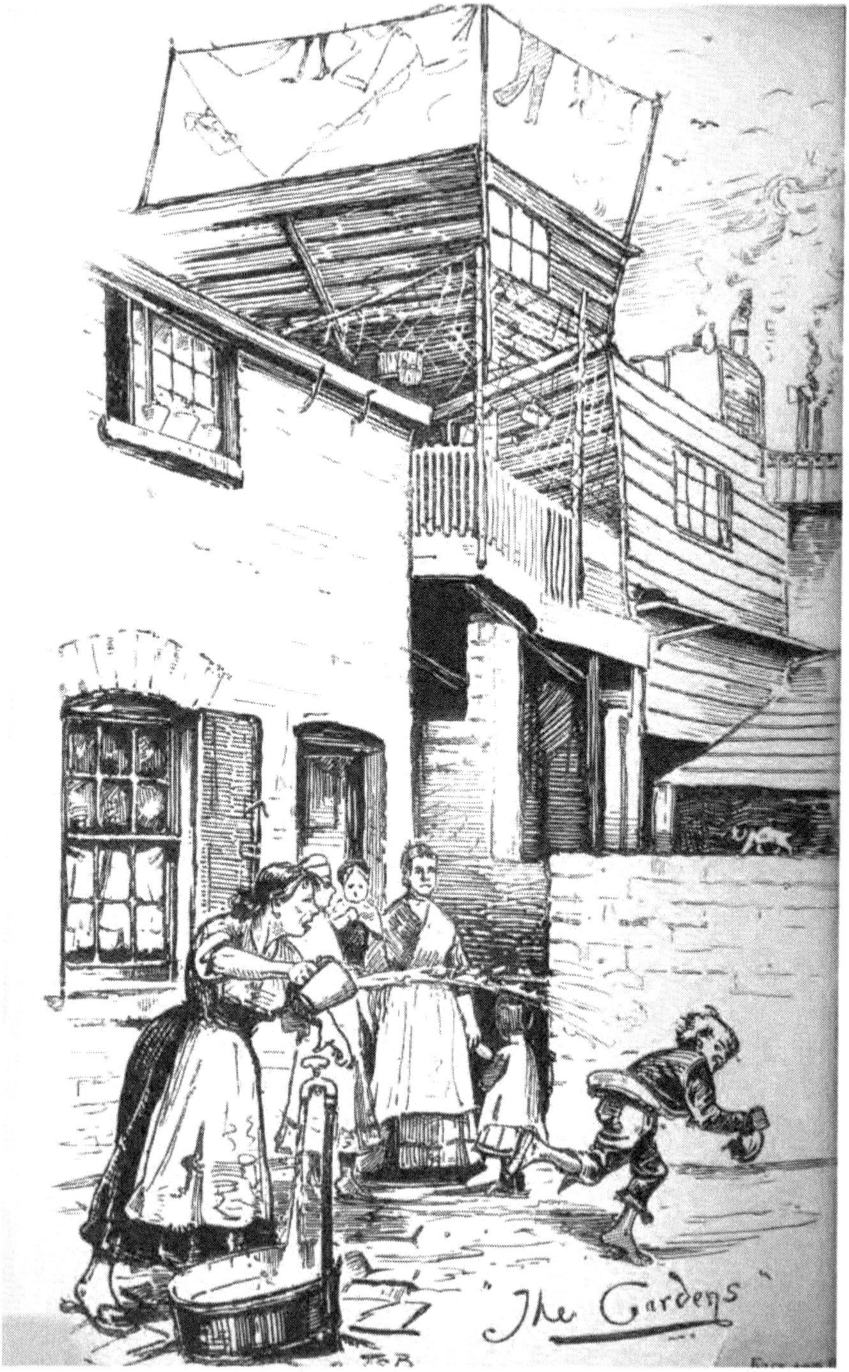
"The Gardens"

a runaway who does not stop to pay his rent. This gentleman was informed that, as the sum of three pounds sterling was then due on his account to his landlord therein named, certain chattels had been seized, as specified thereunder, and which in the inventory were briefly thus described: " Four old Chairs, Mixed bed, and Shaving-glass."

What may be a "mixed " bed, the reader must be left to guess. I have no suggestion to help him in the matter, save that when a clown puts on his nightcap in a panto-mime, the bed is pretty sure to get "a little mixed." And indeed the notion of the Law, in all its solemn majesty, being set to work to sell up all the goods of Mr. Glibbery, might well appear suggestive of a first-rate comic scene.

A thought of something humorous is worth having in the East, where the traveller will find his spirits easily de-pressed. So the tableau of the Sheriff entering to slow music (to indicate the tardy progress of the Law), and seizing the four old chairs, and the mixed bed and the shaving-glass, formed a pleasant subject for a mental picture, to occupy our fancy as we went upon our way. The next halt that we came to was made in certain (so-called) Gardens, which had nothing horti-cultural about them, save their name. No hyacinths grew here, nor any sprig of green, and the only thing approaching to a fir-tree was a clothes'-prop. The gardens formed a no-thoroughfare, with a blank wall at the end, and beyond was a canal, and on all sides the horizon, which was not very distant, was monotonous with chimney-pots. Here we had a smiling welcome from a comely little woman, whose cheerful voice and manner formed a pleasant contrast to the dreariness around her. As we entered, she was busy giving dinner to her baby, who appeared to relish highly the plentiful maternal nourishment. Three cleanly little girls were clustered by the fire, with a cat by way of plaything somewhere in their midst. Two larger girls were absent—at school, their mother said, and she likewise owned a boy, who, like his father, was at work. There were some ugly china "ornaments" paraded on the chimney-piece, and, in the way of higher art, there was displayed a coloured photograph of General Garibaldi, to be recognised quite readily by his prominent red shirt. On the shelves to right and left of him there was a goodly show of crockery, which she said she had bought cheap, for it was given with the tea; and, to complete the household luxuries, there were a leash of clocks. These, however, were "all cripples," said the cheery little woman; but her husband had a weakness for seeing clocks about him, though they weren't of any use.

Four shillings a week was the rent paid for their house—for this room of ten square feet, say, and for the bedroom over it. This latter we were shown by the little dame in person, still carrying her baby, who was still at his repast. The stairs were steep but clean, and the chamber, though not large, looked quite palatial in appointment, as compared with all the other sleeping-places we had seen. There was actually a carpet in it, not a very large one, it is true, but still a carpet; and there was another clock, and this was really going; and there was a little table—let us say a toilette-table, for a clothes-brush lay upon it; and there was a bed with sheets and counterpane—yes, real sheets and counterpane; and by the window, curtained off, was a small bed for the son, and a bed, a trifle bigger, was there for the five little daughters by the door.

Everything seemed clean and neat, above stairs and below. The house looked poor, no doubt, but still there was some comfort in it. "Ah," exclaimed the little mistress as baby ended his repast, "ah, it weren't always like this, now was it, Mr. Austin? Difference? Why yes, it's made a difference in all ways, both to him and me too. There, he'll work from morn to midnight now he will, and never grumble not one bit he won't. And he gives me all he gets too, an' I can feed the children well now, an' keep 'em clothed, an' tidy like. And I never could do that, you know, an' we was mostly all'ys glumpy afore he took the pledge."

I found, by further questioning the cheery little woman, that her husband was a sort of clever Jack-of-all-trades, who "did up houses" here and there and anywhere, she said, and was able by so doing, working late and early, to earn a pound or so a week. He seemed well-nigh a Crœsus, when compared with all the wretchedly-paid workers I had heard of, and had seen too, in the East. But perhaps his calling needed more than common brain-work; more, for instance, than a costermonger's, which chiefly needs good lungs.

By way of a sad contrast to this cheerful little soul and her children, who, with baby, might have warbled, "We are Seven," we found a family next door who were terribly afflicted by the badness of the times, which has long been an epidemic ailment in the East. The mother we had met just as we left the caravan She was trying to earn a sixpence by the selling of her "creeses," and was tying them in farthing bundles as she briskly trudged along. "Hard at work? Well, yes, sir," as we exchanged a greeting. "One had need to work hard nowadays, if one don't want to starve." She seemed a bustling, active, clean-cheeked, civil-speaking body, who tried to make the best of things, and had seen better days. Her shoes were in holes, and she was very poorly clad, and there was a worn and anxious look upon her face. That this was not without a cause became pretty clear to me, when I had seen her home and the children she was toiling for, out there in the wet street.

Their father was at work too; making fish-baskets he was, and when in luck's way he could do a tidy trade. Make a couple of gross a day he could, and more too if he stuck to it and didn't stop a minute 'cept for swallowing of his meals. Profit? Well, he reckoned he could make four bob a day a'most, but then you had to

The clock mender's family

"Creeses."

a-making fish-baskets he was

J. B

go and sell 'em fust, and that was mostly
a day's work. But the worst of it was
as you couldn't get the stuff, now the
sugar-trade were slack, leastways down
there in the East.

The obvious connection between fish-
baskets and sugar not being apparent to
my uncommercial mind, it was explained
that the baskets were made of the rush
wrappers wherein the raw sugar was sent
to be refined. Since this business had
been sorely crippled by the foreign
bounties, the basket-maker suffered no less
than the sugar-baker from the want of
work. My voluble informant had but one
eye, and he kept this keenly fixed on me
while he imparted his instruction; as a
schoolman sharply notices the dulness of a
dunce. Having done his best to enlighten
my crass ignorance, he left his basket-
making (which was done al fresco, in a
drizzle and a draught), and showed the
way indoors. A wretched room it was,
this sitting-room or kitchen—call it which
one pleased, the name would scarce be fit.
For there was not a scrap of fire, nor any
sign of cookery past, present, or to come;
and, for purposes of sitting, there were but
two old chairs, one with a broken leg.
Floor and ceiling were in holes, and the
plaster in great patches had crumbled from
the walls. A pale-cheeked little boy, with
the thinnest threadbare clothing to cover
his thin limbs, was nursing a sick child,
wrapped up in an old petticoat; while
another boy, still smaller and still more
thinly clad, was—playing, shall I say ?—
with a remarkably lean cat. A bit or two

of crockery lay huddled in a corner, and
the only ornament displayed was an old
discarded horse-shoe, which, the man said,
with grim irony, was hanging there "for
luck."

Upstairs we found two beds, one with a
patched coverlet and but little underneath
it; and the other with some scanty bits of
sackcloth to cover its defects. In these
two beds the parents and their half-dozen
children (five boys and a girl) contrived
somehow to sleep. Possibly, for warmth's
sake, close quarters were endurable; for
the walls seemed hardly weather-tight, and
in the ceiling also the bare laths were
revealed. "Well, yes, it do drip through a
bit," the man was free to own, after telling
us that he paid four shillings weekly for his
rent, and that the landlord had promised
to look to the repairs. "Look to 'em?
Well, yes, you see, he do look in a' times
and give us a look round. But if we so
much as p'ints to 'em, he 'ooks it pretty
quick."

One of the window-panes was broken,
and mended with a bit of newspaper,
which, however, hardly served to keep the
wind out. I remarked that as the room
was little more than ten feet square, and
there were nightly eight to sleep in it,
perhaps it was as well to have a little
ventilation. Plenty of fresh air was a
famous thing for health, and there was
nothing so unwholesome as a close and
stuffy bedchamber.

"Well, sir," observed the man with
rather a grim smile, "I don't think as you'd
much complain o' feeling stuffy if you was

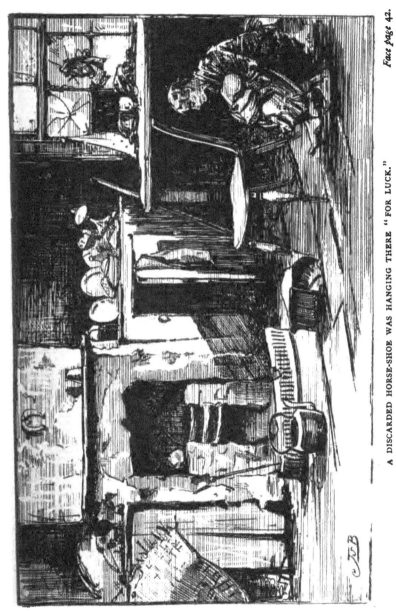

A DISCARDED HORSE-SHOE WAS HANGING THERE "FOR LUCK."

Face page 42.

to sleep here a bit. We ain't in want of air, scarce, with a door as hardly shuts and a windy as half closes. Nor yet we ain't much short o' water neither, leastways when it rains we ain't, with a roof as is half rotten and about as full o' holes as an old collander. An' were a jolly good frost to come, we wouldn't be over warm neither. Ah, you may well say it's a blessing that we're having a mild winter. If it had been a hard one, God knows what would ha' become of us. It's a precious bad time that we're a having as it is, but if we've a month's frost you'd better put me in my coffin. I ain't a lazybones, I ain't, nor yet a lie-a-bed, I ain't neither, now am I, Mr. Austin? You've knowed me for some years now, and you ain't catched me a skylarkin', no, nor 'yet a lushin' neither, not but what I likes a drop o' beer when I've been workin' 'ard and I've a few spare coppers 'andy. But it's precious few they are just now, and tidy hard to get, and a pint o' beer's as sca'ce here as a pinch o' baccy."

I asked him how he earned his livelihood when he could not get the stuff for fish-baskets; whether, for instance, he had ever been working at the docks, and whether there was much of a scramble for admittance, for I had heard of a man being sadly hurt while in the crowd there. "Shouldn't wonder, sir," he answered. "You see it's this way, just at present. There's a hunderd of 'em waiting, and there's forty or so wanted. An' the weak 'uns gets the wall, and the strong 'uns gets the work. Seen 'em? Yes; I've seen 'em

and I've been among 'em too, scores an'
scores o' times, I have. It's a reg'lar knock
me down for labour is the docks. And
what with all the waitin', I declare, sir, it
don't pay. It's heart-breakin', it is, to
stan' there 'most all day, an' never get a
job, and then come home without a copper,
and find the children all a cryin' and a
sobbin' for their supper, and most like they
an' their mother too ain't 'ad not a mouth-
ful nor a mossel, not since yest'day. Work?
Look here, sir, I ain't afraid o' work, nor I
ain't no ways proud neither. In the way
of a day's work, I'd put my hand a'most to
anythin'; Mr. Austin 'll tell you that, sir.
Yes, an' there's thousands such as me, too,
down here in the East, there is. An' what
I says, as it's hard lines on a man as have
a family to keep, an' is willin' enough to
work for 'em, and then to go from week's
end unto week's end, an' not get none."

Here my guide mildly interposed a hint
that State-helped Emigration perhaps might
prove a remedy, by ridding the East End
of its surplusage of labour. "But look
here, Mr. Austin, it's like this way," said
the basket-maker. "The more there goes
away, the more there comes to fill the gaps.
See here now, sir. Last month about five
hundred was shipped off to Horsetrailier.
Well, thinks I, a good riddance. There'll
be fewer mouths to fill, and fewer hands to
work here now. But last week there come
about a thousand from abroad, an' they all
landed at the docks, an' here they seem to
stick, and it's mostly Polish Jews they
are."

The few last words he added with something of a snort, as though the creed and foreign country had made the grievance worse, and the presence of these immigrants in Stepney still more odious. Perhaps his temper might have led him to speak harshly of the strangers, whose arrival he lamented, had not my guide enquired if he were coming to the Hall next Sunday morning. "Well," replied the basket-maker, with as straightforward a look as his one eye would allow him, " I'd be willin' enough to come an' hear a bit o' gospel. It all'ys seem to do me good, and make me feel the better, though perhaps I mayn't quite rightly understand it. Though you seem to put it plain, too; I'm not denyin' that, sir. But you see, sir, I ain't proud, still I ain't one to be sneered at. Now, just see this old coat o' mine. It's the on'y one I got, and there ain't much of a go-to-meetin' sort of cut about it. I don't think as you'd fancy being seen in it o' Sundays, an' 'specially by daylight."

There was a twinkle in his eye as he said this, which seemed the outward sign of much inward hilarity. "But, sir," continued he, "my missus, she'll be there. She all'ys somehow manages to rig herself up tidy, though she ain't one to spend a farden upon finery. But she's all'ys neat, she is, leastways on a Sunday. An' she'll come in the morning, sir, 'cause one of us must stay at home to mind the little 'uns. And—well, yes—perhaps you'll see me in the evening, 'cause after dark, you know, an old coat ain't much noticed."

Ah, my friend, thought I, as I shook

him by the hand, on bidding him farewell, many a well-off man makes many a worse excuse for not going to morning service, than the want which you allege of a decent coat to go in.

Leaving, then, the basket-maker to look after his children, while seeing also to his work, as well as his one eye could perform the double labour, we emerged from the Gardens which had been so wrongly named, and continued to explore the wilderness of brickwork wherewith we were encompassed. But we had hardly proceeded fifty paces on our way, when suddenly my guide exclaimed——

Alas! my sheet is full, and I can only beg the reader, who would hear this sudden outcry, to wait for my next paper.

TRAVELS IN THE EAST.

PART III.*

"You ought to see the Smoke Holes!"
This was the exclamation wherewith I had so suddenly been startled by my guide, shortly after we had left our friend the one-eyed basket-maker, who, by a funny freak of memory, somehow had reminded me of the one-eyed Second Calender in the Arabian Nights. The dear Arabian Nights! For how many pleasant days have I to thank those precious Nights! What magical delights have been conjured by their spell! Like orient pearls at random strung, these gems of Eastern fairy lore have been fastened on my memory, and in many a dark hour have flashed upon my brain. How I have pitied poor Aladdin when his palace disappeared, and with it his fair princess, whose long name Badroulbadour no schoolboy dare pronounce; and how I have rejoiced when she so pluckily had poisoned the magician, and Aladdin had regained possession of his lamp! How I have envied Camaralzaman the love of his Badoura, and have enjoyed the ducking of his servant in the well! How sorry I have felt for the young king of the Black Isles, who from the

* ALL THE YEAR ROUND, March, 15, 1884.

waist downwards was marble, and not
man! How I have read with breathless
interest every detail of the battle fought
between the Queen of Beauty and the
Evil Genius, who, appearing as a lion, was
halved neatly by a hair (transformed into
a scythe), then was changed into a scor-
pion, a serpent, a pussy-cat, and a pome-
granate-seed, and after escaping as a fish
from the jaws of his pursuer, rose from the
water all aflame, and was burned finally
to bits! How I have laughed at poor
Alnaschar, the barber's fifth brother, when
he kicked over his glass-ware, and
awoke from his sweet day-dream of
prosperity and pomp! How I have
longed to have a mount on the Enchanted
Horse, and to go with Prince Firouz
Schah, that boldest of all high-flyers, on a
flight towards the moon! I remember,
when I climbed a tree to peep into a
pigeon's nest, I often pleased myself with
thinking how young Sindbad the Sailor
had discovered the roc's egg by a similar
ascent; or how dear old Ali Baba, being
similarly perched, heard the magical
"Open Sesame" of the famous Forty
Thieves. I believe I could still find, on
the sea-shore nigh to Felixstowe, the
precise spot where the fisherman, to my
fancy, was at work when the Genius (the
"Genie" in my old, ill-printed version) was
escaping wrapped in smoke from the yellow
copper vase; and I could readily show the
place in the quaint old town of Harwich
where Aladdin saw the princess coming
from her bath. The dear Arabian Nights!
As Talleyrand exclaimed, "Ah, what a

The "Smoke-holes"

J.S.B

Face page 48.

sad old age you are preparing for yourself!" to a young man who protested that he cared not to learn whist; so would I cry out, "Ah, what lifelong pleasures of memory you may lose if you care not in your youth to read the dear Arabian Nights!"

But I have mounted on my hobby-horse, and am galloping away from the guidance of my guide, who had suddenly exclaimed to me:

"Now we are so near them, you ought to see the smoke - holes." The smoke-holes? Why yes, certainly. Since he thought it was my duty, I would surely see the smoke-holes. As a traveller, I was bound to see the strange sights of the country I was bent upon exploring. The smoke-holes? What on earth they were, I could not imagine. There was a magic in their name that whetted curiosity, and made me anxious to behold these marvels of the East.

As we trudged along, my fancy revelled in the smoke-holes. Were they geysers, or volcanoes, or deep caverns in the earth; fissures sulphurous and ghastly, vomiting huge volumes of vaporous obscurity, Smoke - holes like to these seemed suggested by my memories of Oriental fairy-tale and scenes described in travellers' books. But the reality fell short of the preconceived romance.

We found the smoke - holes simply chimneys, square-built of thick planks, about four feet in width, and a dozen or so in height. In each a fire of sawdust lay smouldering at bottom, while above hung sprats or haddocks, regular in rows, and

spitted upon sticks. A "machine" of fish,
I learned, was a truck-load of two tons;
and such were often bought and shared
among the renters of the smoke-holes,
whose trade it was to clean, and salt, and
dry, and smoke the fish. In the shed
which we had entered, a couple of men
were busily employed in splitting haddocks
at a most amazing pace; cleaning them
and sorting them according to their sizes,
and a little too, it seemed to me, according
to their smell. Another man and a small
boy were opening their gills, and stringing
them on sticks, which they hung across the
holes. Above the heads of the two
splitters, in a cage six inches square, a
pretty little linnet was warbling to the
workers, who seemed to have small leisure
to listen to his song.

In the yard next door, a man and boy
were likewise hard at work, spitting sprats
upon the sticks. This seemed a work more
delicate and slower to accomplish, as they
were smaller fish. They looked silvery and
bright as they were taken from the salting
tub. In the room through which we passed
—and which seemed scullery, and kitchen,
and dining-room, and workshop, and bed-
chamber to boot—two women, brisk and
buxom, with their sleeves tucked to their
elbows, were employed in cleaning similar
small fish. A cat lay snoozing by the fire,
looking comfortably sleek, and presenting
a rare contrast to the lean cats we had
seen. She was doubtless fond of fish—
pussies generally are—although I guessed
her to be a new comer, for she must have had
a glut of it in such a fishy place. However

Splitting haddocks

Salting

good her appetite, she must soon feel like
the grocer's boy, who finds that sugar is
too sweet for him after a week's work.

I remarked upon the number of what I
mistook for mice-holes, in the flooring by
the hearthstone, and the corners of the
walls. I said I thought the cat must be
neglectful of her duty, and was hardly
worth her keep; she looked so sleek and
sleepy, and the mice seemed so abundant.
"Mices 'oles!" cried the woman, smiling
at my ignorance. "Law, sir, they ain't
mices 'oles, they're rats' 'oles, that's what
they are. An' a plenty of 'em we has too, an'
can't no ways keep 'em out, we can't. Fast
as ever we blocks one 'ole, there they makes
another bigger. They're too sharp for the
cat to catch, and as for settin' o' traps, it
ain't a mite of use. Bait 'em as you may,
they won't never go anigh 'em. I s'pose
as it's the hoffle as temps 'em to flock in so.
Y'see, sir, after a goodish spell o' work,
an' speshly cleanin' 'addocks, there's allys
lots o' hoffle, and I fancy as the rats they
likes it for their suppers. Bless you, when
the light's out, and there's nobody to see
'em, 'cause they're 'mazin' shy is rats, they
cuts out of their 'oles, and kicks up such a
caper! One can't hardly sleep a' times,
they're so a squealin', an' a squeakin', an' a
kickin' up a shindy. Nuisance? Well yes,
now you come to think of it, they are a
slightish nuisance. I've often felt 'em on
the bed, and 'ad to keep a stick anigh me
'andy for to knock 'em off it. More nor
once or twice they've runned over acrost
my face they have, and my 'usband says
he've eered 'em a gnawrin' of his whiskies.

Why yes, you may say that, sir. 'Tis well as they likes fish, or some fine night they'd be a nibblin' of our noses off."

A very little boy, with very little clothing on, was prattling to his mother, while he played about the room. He had no playmate to help him, nor had he any plaything, and he seemed playing a small game of hide-and-seek all by himself. His cheeks were plump and rosy—they were the first Eastern roses I had seen—and he looked certainly as though a fish diet agreed with him, as it did clearly with the cat. To vary the monotony of his playing all alone, I took him by the arms, and gave him the delight of some jumping in the air. He seemed mightily to relish this new form of entertainment; and, when I bade good-bye to him, he eyed me rather wistfully, much as a dog may eye his master when the dog desires to be taken for a walk. Chancing to look round when I was half-way down the street, I perceived my young playmate closely following at my heels, and he began to cry a little when his mother called him back. Well, thought I, as he left me, it is an easy thing to please a child who wants a game of play; and this little fellow can certainly have known but little pleasure in his life, when he finds so much enjoyment in a few jumps from the floor.

There are plenty of these smoke-holes to be met with in the East; and some few of their occupants appear now to be doing a fairly thriving trade, in comparison, at least, with other Eastern folk. In using the word "occupants," I write a little

figuratively, for certainly the occupation of
a smoke - hole would be anything but
pleasant, and hardly even possible with
the sawdust well alight. Some amount of
capital must certainly be needful to enable
a few traders to buy two tons of fish.
Indeed, I heard some whispers floating
somewhere in the air, about the fortunes
that were rumoured to be stored up in old
stockings, or otherwise concealed. But I
fancy there are middlemen with fingers in
the pie, who help themselves, no doubt, to
a good slice of its contents. The fish-
markets are in a rather fishy state at
present, and if some few among the smokers
somehow manage in some years to put by
something handsome, they do so by hard
working at a rather ugly trade.

It must be understood, moreover, that
many of these fish-curers are compelled to
live by piecework, for they are far too poor
to share in buying a "machine." As the
work is intermittent, and comes by sudden
fits and starts, it can hardly be regarded as
a regular employment. Indeed, in a slack
season there are many workless, and therefore wageless days; and at such times it is
difficult, if not impossible, for any man to
earn above a crown or so a week.

We had scarcely left the smoke-holes,
and the scent of certain sprats was still
fresh in our nostrils—though "fresh,"
perhaps, is hardly the right adjective to
use—when we were suddenly enveloped in
an odour far more savoury, whereof a few
sniffs called to mind the fragrant smell of
Irish stew. Quickly following our noses,
we traced the perfume to a pint mug which

was wrapped in an old handkerchief, and was being carried, by a poor newly-widowed woman, home to her sick child. The stew had clearly come from the Cottage Mission kitchen, for where else was procurable, at least in that poor neighbourhood, such richly smelling food? Now the mission stew was made, as I well knew, "to be consumed upon the premises," and was "supplied in their own jugs," or plates, to its consumers, who were allowed to eat their fill there, but to carry none away. This was the rule, and very sensible it was. My guide, however, now informed me that, in case of serious illness, the rule was not made absolute, and that children or their mothers were very properly allowed to take away a helping, if they had a little one lying sick at home. Of the good done by these dinners I had already taken count, and here was further proof of how they were esteemed. This poor woman had been walking for a mile or two, and waiting for an hour or so, to get a little wholesome food to carry home. Her little girl had hardly yet recovered from the whooping-cough, and was so weak, the doctor said, that she must have some meat. Perhaps he might as well have prescribed a slice of peacock, or an ortolan or two, or a pine-apple, or a peach. How was a poor widow to buy meat, she'd like to know, when she'd four children to feed, and with all her slaving only earned five bob a week? For despite of all the advertised advantages of machines, stitching shirts is still a starvation sort of work, and the wages to be gained are little higher than they were when the famous song about it was first put into print.

The next halt that we made was in the house of a poor woman, a widow like the last, and like her a hard worker, and one who very literally had hard work to live, while living by hard work. She was idle now, however, for she had sprained her back, and so her daughter, somehow, managed to do the work of both. And it wasn't easy neither, to make fifty beds a day, leastways forty-seven, if you'd like to speak exact, besides a cleaning of the rooms and a sweeping of the stairs a bit. An' then there was a washing every week of fifty, leastways of forty-seven sheets, and a score or so of towels—not little 'uns, neither, mind you, but regular big jacks. This was the hard labour to which she and her daughter had been condemned, perhaps for life, or at any rate for a living. A certain poor men's lodging-house just down there in the Causeway, was the place where this life punishment was being so worked out. Nine shillings a week was all the wages they could earn, and there were three mouths besides her own to fill.

Eighteenpence a week was the rent of the reception-room wherein we were received. We found it was, in fact, the rent of the whole house. Explored from ground to roof, the mansion held no other chamber ; indeed, so tumbledown a house it was that hardly it held this. I could scarcely say with truth that we were in a downstairs room ; for staircase there was none, and no attempt at a first floor. The walls seemed thin and tottering ; and, if they

did not let the air in, it entered pretty freely
through the window and the door. There
were big holes in the ceiling which served
to admit daylight ; big holes were visible
likewise in the roof. Perhaps for a day-
worker this might be esteemed a benefit,
for the window was a small one, and the
glass was much begrimed. A smell of
something filthy, and likewise something
smoky, seemed to hang about the place,
and as there was no fire there, I confidently
guessed it must be coming from outside.

"You're about right, sir," replied the
poor widow. "It comes in through the
window and down the chimney too, and
mayhap through the roof a bit. You see,
they're burning tins down in the yard
yonder, and when the tins are extry foul,
the smoke is apt to stink."

I peeped through the dim casement as
well as I was able ; and not far off I saw,
all piled up in big heaps, a mountainous
range of tins of differing formation, and
varying antiquity, all mingled in a chaos
that would certainly have puzzled a savant
to have sketched. There were biscuit-tins,
and flour-tins, and paraffin-tins, and colza-
tins, and sardine-tins, and candle-tins, and
tins of half-a-hundred shapes, and sorts,
and sizes, whose past uses were quite past
my present powers to explain. They were
different in shape and different in substance,
and in one thing only they seemed to be
alike. All were old, and all were dirty,
and most of them most foul, and all were
there awaiting some strange purifying process, which seemed not very odorous, to
sweeten their fouled substance into some-

"You gets the Key o' the street
instead o' the front door you does."

thing useable, when seen in a re-melted and re-modelled state.

Half filling the small room was a bed with an old counterpane and some little substance under it. What that substance was, whether hay, or straw, or horsehair, I did not care to ask. It really seemed too little to be of much account. Nor did I care to guess how the mother and three children could all sleep in that one bed. Unless the latter were extremely small, they must have found it a tight fit.

A cat mewed at the door, and her mistress let her in. Puss wore a shabby coat of black and dirty white, which sadly needed to be washed. Nor was her personal appearance improved in other points. Her tail was out of curl, and her whiskers were unbrushed, and there were traces of a gutter tramp left sticking to her feet. She seemed indeed too hungry to attend much to her toilette, and I almost doubted if she were in her right mind. A cat of any common-sense would have surely left a place where she appeared so little cared for, and this specimen seemed indeed to be half starved.

"I foun' her in the street one night, nigh Bromley," said the widow. "It were a drizzlin' a bit, and there were a east wind blowin' enough to blow your 'at off, and she were a mewing piteous she was. So I wrapped her in my apron, and carried her straight 'ome with me. An' here she have lived since, though it ain't much of a living. Well now, I dessay you may think I can't afford to keep a cat much. But there, she don't cost nothin'. I never buy no milk

for her, nor meat neither, for that matter.
An' you know, sir, she grows all her own
clothing, and she ain't like my boy Billy,
'cause she don't wear out no boots. She
catches of her mice somewheres; it ain't
here, for we've got none. There's nothin'
for 'em to eat, so they're wise to keep away
from 'ere. Well yes, sir, she ain't much of
a beauty, but I'd be sorry to lose her, that
I would. You see, she's company like, she
is, and is somethin' as one can talk to
when one's feeling a bit lonesome, an' the
children ain't at home. An' then they
likes to play with her they does, and it
ain't much one's got to play with, you
know, sir, when one's poor."

I remarked upon the bad state of repair
in which the house was kept, and suggested
that the roof did not seem wholly water-
tight. "Well no, sir, I can't say as it do,"
replied the widow, with something like
the ghost of a dead smile on her wan face:
"What with all them 'oles, and the plaster
off the ceiling, we often wants an umbe-
rella a'most to keep the rain off. Yes,
I've spoken to the landlord, and he tells
me as he'll see to it. And so peraps he
may—leastways, if he live long enough.
Oh yes, sir, he's well off enough. One of
the pious ones he is, and goes to service
regular. He looks sharpish for his rents,
though, an' he don't give 'em away much;
leastways, about here he don't. The
Parish ought to know, you say? Law
bless you, who's the Parish? You see,
the 'ouse is tidy cheap, as 'ouses go, an' if
I was to leave I mightn't find another
easy. And there, it never ain't no good

Miss Napton.

Face page 59.

to pick a quarrel with your landlord. You gets the key o' the street, instead o' the front door, you does. The 'ouse ain't over water-tight, nor wind-tight neither, mind you; but it's better than none, an' one mustn't be too pertickler when one can't afford it."

With this philosophic aphorism to refresh me in my travels, I took my leave of the good widow, whom I mentally commended for the brave attempt she made to seem content with her hard lot. After making a few more halts upon my way, and traversing a mile or more of brick-work so monotonous, by thoroughfares so similar, that I wondered how my guide could find his way along them, we returned to Salmon Lane, where there was business that awaited him. Among other news, Miss Napton, the kind lady-super-intendent, reported a visit she had made the day before, which had very much distressed her. Calling just at nightfall on a family hard-by, she found the mother and her children anxiously expecting the home-coming of the father, who was a dock-labourer. He presently returned, looking sorely worn and haggard. "Look here," he cried half savagely, flinging his hat upon the floor; "I've been a tryin' hard all day, an' haven't earned a blessed farden. I been a standin' at the gates, an' a trampin' through the streets, till it's right down faint I am. And God A'mighty knows what we're to do to-morrow to keep ourselves from starving."

"Oh," exclaimed the kindly visitor, "if you had but heard the cry that those poor hungry children gave, when they found their father hadn't brought home food for them, I declare you must almost have cried yourself, as I did. But I hurried home at once and sent them a loaf of bread ; and so, poor little things, they didn't sleep quite supperless."

I bade my guide good-bye, after hearing this sad story, and promising ere long to resume my Eastern travels. As I trudged home through the City, I entered the Cathedral. How lofty and how noble appeared its spacious dome, compared with all the mean and wretched rooms I had been visiting ! The organ was just pealing forth the grandest of its tones, and the chubby, clean-cheeked, white-robed little choristers were sweetly carolling their evensong of thanksgiving and praise. Ah, thought I, my young friends, you may well sing " Oh, be joyful ! " How many are your joys, and how few can be your griefs ! Well catered for, well clad, and well cared for as you are, what a contrast are your lives to those of the poor children whose mothers starve at shirt-making, and who go supperless to bed when their fathers get no work !

TRAVELS IN THE EAST.

PART IV.*

It was on the morning of Ash Wednesday that I was able to resume my journey in the East; a proper day, I thought, whereon to mortify the flesh by taking a long tramp.

As I jumped into the train that took me to my trysting-place, I somehow fell into a train of sentimental thought. It may have been suggested by some salt-fish in a window, as I approached the station. But, whatever was its origin, there arose the meditation that many an idle lounger, who lolls about the West, might, by way of Lenten penance, do well to make a pilgrimage some fine day to the East. If it were a wet day, the penance might be greater, but the walking might be less. Worn out sight-seer though he were, he would behold a novel sight or two, and some perhaps might make him stare; and, though reflection is fatiguing, some might even make him think.

To one who leads a life of luxury and ease, it must seem a strange idea to have to slave in a back slum, and scarce get bread enough to eat. The point "Is life

---

* ALL THE YEAR ROUND, March 22, 1884.

worth living ?" may be put before a Sybarite, who deems it a hard labour to strike a match in order to light a cigarette; but it certainly presents a very different aspect when viewed by a poor shirtmaker, who, to save herself from starving, must daily work for fifteen hours at a stretch. A man who chiefly spends his time between his stable and his club, might haply get a trifle of his selfishness shamed out of him, if he were to pay a penitential visit to the East, and see the sort of lives that his fellow-men are living, and the sort of dwellings wherein they have to live.

With some few thoughts like these to beguile me on my way, I set forth on my day's travel; and shortly after noon I met my punctual guide at the appointed place. We had not proceeded far, when something led me to remark that I wished to see the rooms of some of those poor sempstresses, of whom there had been told such pitiable tales. "Nothing is more easy," he replied, "there are plenty of them hereabouts," and well-nigh directly, on rounding the next corner, we entered a small street which, as it bore the name of an Eastern bird of prey, conveyed a covert reference to the sellers of cheap slop-work, made by starving of the poor.

Here, in a small house—though I need hardly use the epithet, for in the East there are none large—we climbed a few steep stairs, and knocked at a small door. This we found on the first-floor; at least it would have been the first-floor, if there had been a second, and an answer to our knock bade us cheerily, "come in." We

"Buttons are a bother"

The machinist and her baby

Face page 63

were welcomed very heartily by a pleasant-
looking woman, in the poorest of poor
clothes, who was "machining" at a table
that stood beneath the window; a small
bedstead being opposite, close beside the
door. Her machine was on the table, and
there likewise was her baby—a thin and
solemn baby, sitting quite sedately in a
very tiny chair, and staring silently at
mother while she pursued her work. A
curly, light-haired little boy was standing
by her side; and in spite of all his ragged-
ness he really would have looked a very
pretty little fellow, but for the sore skin
that showed the poorness of his blood. He
was trying to make playthings of two little
bits of firewood, to which, in shape of cat-
o'-nine-tails, he had tied some scraps of
tape. The cheapest of cheap clocks was
ticking on the mantelpiece, and a small
kettle was simmering beside a smaller fire,
but neither of these noises stood a chance of
interfering with the sound of the machine.
Piled upon a chair, and put quite ready
to her hand, lay a lot of little pieces
of thickish grey tweed cloth, shaped as the
two sides of what in the cheap clothing
lists are recorded as "boys' vests." These
were to be sewn, and neatly fitted to the
back, and in point of fact the garment,
button-holes excepted, was to be sewn
throughout.

Buttons! Oh yes, certainly. She had
to put the buttons on, and to press the
work, when finished. And she also had to
pay for the hire of the machine, and to buy
her needles too, she had, and pay for her
own thread. Sewing pretty steadily from

seven in the morning until nine or so at night, merely stopping for her meals, and not long neither for them, she could manage pretty well to make three waist-coats in a day, and she was paid sometimes sixpence, sometimes sevenpence apiece.

That was all they could depend on just at present for their living, because her husband, a dock labourer, could scarcely get any work. Tried his uttermost, he did, she was sure of that, but there, you know, luck didn't always come to them who wanted it the most. Shirts? Yes, she'd made shirts; but it really didn't pay, scarce. Starvation sort o' work it was, a'most as bad as making match-boxes. You had to machine 'em when shaped out, and do 'em regular right through, you had, excep' the button-'oles, you know; and there was, well, a stiffish bit o' stitchin' in a dozen shirts. And you had to find your needles and your cotton, too, you had, and that, you know, would come to close on twopence-farthing, or even twopence-halfpenny, 'cause both thread and needles, too, they often would get broke, when the stuff were extry stiff. And there, a shilling a dozen was all as you could get for 'em, so you scarce earned more nor ninepence by a hardish day o' work.

Her statement was interrupted at this point by the arrival of a visitor, who entered without knocking, as though her visits were too frequent to need any announcement. She was rather a pretty girl, with features small and delicate; and she might have looked much prettier had her cheeks been somewhat plumper and a shade less pale. She was very plainly clothed in an old dress of thin material, which in respect of thinness was suited to her figure. Her voice was rather thin too, and high-pitched in its tone, as though it had been sharpened to a business sort of point. She spoke quite pleasantly, however, and her words were well pronounced, with no cockneyfied misuse of the eighth letter of the alphabet; but with a certain briskness which showed that she was capable of speaking her own mind.

On her entrance she exchanged a friendly greeting with my guide, whom she seemed much pleased to see. He called her by her christian-name, having known her from her childhood, and she had long been a good helper to him in his mission-work.

Soon letting her tongue loose, as though it needed exercise, and this five minutes' leisure were too rare a treat to miss, she replied to all my questions well-nigh ere they were put. Her age was twenty-one, she owned without a scruple, although she hardly would be thought as much, except for her worn face. A hard worker all the week, she worked hard at the Sunday-school, where she had herself been taught most of the knowledge she possessed. She was living with her mother, as she had done all her life, and she didn't mean to leave her, though it wasn't altogether what you'd think an easy life. Machining all day long isn't what you'd call quite fancy needlework, you know, such as ladies like to do when they're tired of sitting idle. Ah yes, she was often tired of sitting, but she'd never had the chance of getting tired of being idle. How long would it take her? Well, she couldn't tell exactly. But it wouldn't take her long to go and have a try.

Briskly taking part in the commercial conversation interrupted by her visit, she added a few details from her own experience. With a rapid stream of words which it was difficult to stem, and which seemed flowing from her heart, she vividly described and vehemently denounced the disadvantages of piecework, so far, at least, as the worker was concerned. "You can do your work at home?" "Oh yes, of course you can. But there's not much good in that when you've your meals to cook, you know, and your fire to pay for, if you can't stand freezing. And there's your candle you must find, and that ain't bought for nothing. Then there's the time you lose in going for your work, and returning it when finished. And you've got to take the tram, for you'd tire yourself to death by walking all the way with a big bundle on your head, and they'd not think you respectable if you didn't wear a bonnet. Well, yes, the tram's only twopence, but every penny counts when you work for such small profit. Then there's the time you lose when you buy your silk or cotton, for you must get it to match the colour of the cloth, and that ain't always easy. But the worst is, you're kept waiting such a time when you want to get your work, and—well, yes—a good deal more, too, when you want to get your money. You see, the foreman won't be hurried, and the clerks they won't be bothered for the

likes of you, you know. Ah, it's tiresome
work that waiting. It's all lost time, you
know, and it ain't pleasure either—and it's
hours and hours maybe before you leave
the warehouse."

I enquired whether she thought that any
difference of creed led to any difference in
the terms of her employers; whether, for
instance, she considered that the Christians
or the Jews were the harder of her taskmasters. She replied, and her reply was
echoed by the woman, as sharing her experience, that Christian and Jew were pretty
much alike, in regard to their capacity
for driving a hard bargain. If there were
a shade of preference, perhaps, upon the
whole, she would rather work for Jews,
for there was less pretence about them.
They didn't much pretend to being better
than they were; and this she thought
could not be said so truly of the people
who belonged to the more popular religion.
Oh no, there was nothing of the Jewess
about her. She didn't look much like
Rebecca Isaacs, did she? But she must say
what she thought, you know. And really
now, as far as their commercial conscience
is concerned in beating down their work-
folk to the lowest of low wages, she
thought—well, yes, since you put it so, she
really thought the Jew was pretty nigh
the better Christian.

Baby, who had sat quite silent in his
chair, and who, indeed, from his lofty
position on the table, appeared to be the
chairman of this little trade-meeting, at
this point of the conference emitted a small
cry, which might have been construed

as a speech, to intimate the need of taking some refreshment. Whereupon his mother stopped her sewing; and the honourable chairman, having left the chair, was taken to her bosom, and the meeting was adjourned, perhaps to the Greek Kalends.

With the vigour of her voice still ringing in our ears, and having a desire to hear some further morsels of her wisdom and experience, we followed the chief speaker to her dwelling, not far distant. Here she introduced me to her mother, a poor widow who lived poorly by her needle, as her chatty child did also. She had two sons besides, one of whom lived with them and helped to pay the rent by doing certain barge-work; her two tiny, tidy, little rooms costing every week just half-a-crown apiece. Her other son, a sailor, had been wrecked on his first voyage, and had brought home precisely sixpence after seven months at sea; whereto, notwithstanding this bad start, he had returned.

The room looked on the whole less badly furnished than the last, and there were several small photographs hung about the chimney-piece, and on it were a (doubtful) china ornament or two, which to Eastern connoisseurs, no doubt, were precious works of art. In one of the small portraits taking by the sun, my guide, after a minute of the deepest meditation, thought he recognised some semblance to a somebody called "Charley," to whom he smilingly accused the girl of having been engaged. Whereto she answered naïvely: "No, no, Mr. Austin, I made love to him perhaps, but I never got engaged to him. Besides," she added, gravely smiling, " he couldn't marry much of me, while he was out of work, and I hadn't saved a sixpence to be settled as my fortune ; and perhaps we should have found you forbidding of the banns, for you know you never would have spared me from the Sunday-school."

Here, to change the subject, which might have led from smiles to tears if she were longer to pursue it, I asked for further details as to her plain needlework ; and I gained more knowledge of the noble art of tailoring than I had ever dreamed of in my latter-day philosophy, or could gather from the wisdom of Sartor Resartus.

Buttons always are a bother, as every man and woman knows. But button-holes, in fact, are a bigger bother still, at least so far as the process of their making is concerned. And button-holes, the girl said, were included in the bargain lately driven by her taskmaster ; and they were to be sewn with silk too, which increased their cost to her. And there were pockets to be sewn, too, in the waistcoats she was making ; and this was extra labour, though she had no extra pay for it. She thought the poor folk of the East were sure of being beaten down when they applied for work. They were known to be half starving, and advantage had been taken of the pitiable fact. She and her mother, by working pretty hard, could make, each of them, a couple of good waistcoats in a day ; and each earned upon the whole about a shilling by her work. Nor would the nether garments yield more profit to the family. For making them outright, button-holes and all, the cloth having been cut out, from sixpence to eightpence was now the current price, and there were a dozen buttons to be sewn on, and the sewer had to find both needles and thread.

After singing us a little solo, as it were, in her high-pitched little voice, about the hardness of her life and the avarice of trade —the Chant of the Cheap Clothes Maker, I might, perhaps, have called it, if I had only tried to string her ˉ phrases into rhythm, and to make them rhyme—the little daughter took a part in a trio, or quartette I may say even (for my own fine bass was heard in it), having for its theme the slavery of slop-work and the scarcity of food. Then she joined her mother in singing a duet, wherein, as in an eclogue, they mutually extolled the virtues of my guide. At length, by way of refrain, the daughter chirruped suddenly : " Well, I know that you've been quite a father both to me and mother. Hasn't he, now, mother ? " To which astounding question mother smilingly assented, though it was patent at a glance that my guide, to say the least, is a score of years her junior.

Leaving this good widow and her cheerful, chatty little daughter to resume their ill-paid labour, we descended from the lowly height of their first-floor, and resumed our Eastern journey through the wilderness of brickwork. After half a mile or so, which seemed well-nigh a league, of its dull wearisome monotony, we at length approached some Buildings, which bore their builder's name ; at least, so one might think, for certainly no other

than the architect himself would have been
proud to put his name to such a dismal-
looking place. The special "building"
that we entered looked hardly like a house.
An out-building one might call it, for it
stood at the row's end; and it appeared so
tumbledown that one wondered how it
stood. The walls were all of wood, and
more than half of it looked rotten; and
they seemed somehow held together by
their contact with the roof. Of one small
storey was the building, like the fabric of
a fairy tale. It possessed, however, a
small piece of ground behind, where lean
fowls could be fattened, which, perhaps,
they rarely were; a real back yard one
might term it, for it barely measured more.
Perhaps on this account the rental of the
mansion and estate reached the formidable
figure of twelve shillings a week.

Bells and knockers are at present luxuries unknown to the poor dwellers in
the East. My guide, however, using his
knuckles, obtained a speedy hearing, and,
cheerily as before, we were bidden to come
in. The mention of the rent demanded
for the mansion, which was thrice as much
as any before stated, had raised my expec-
tations to rather a high pitch, and I was,
therefore, not surprised to find the family
assembled around a good - sized table,
which displayed the unexpected possession
of a table cloth, and the perhaps still less
expected sight of a boiled fowl. Not a
whole one, mind you, but merely her
remains. I learned her gender afterwards,
when I was told her date of birth, and
accidental death. Inasmuch as both her

drumsticks and a fragment of her breast, even, had resisted the attack of no fewer than seven appetites, I concluded that she resembled the old turkey (mentioned by Sam Weller) whose one consolation was, when dying, that he was "werry tough."

The seven appetites belonged to a mother and five children, and a poor old half-blind creature who sat crouching by the chimney-corner, in a chair that seemed a size too large for her spare limbs. I mistook her for the grandmother, till her feeble voice corrected me. "No, sir, I ain't no relative. I'm only a lodger, and a trouble to 'em all. I'm a burden, that's what I am, now as I'm getting blind." "No, no," cried mother heartily, "you're no burden, not a bit of it. There, don't you go a whimperin', there's a dear good soul. There ain't nothin' to whimper for, 'cause you ain't a mite of trouble to us. And you needn't think about it now my husbin's in full work again."

These few kindly words appeared to cheer the poor old woman, whose spirits seemed depressed by the dinner she had eaten—perhaps, indeed, the fowl had been too tough for her old teeth. I somehow guessed that, though a lodger, she paid nothing for her rent, and next to nothing for her keep. Indeed, how could she, poor old soul, nearly blinded as she was, earn anything to pay?

Untidy though it was, and littered everywhere with "orts"—which Dr. Johnson has defined to be "things left or thrown away," and has furthermore declared to be an obsolete expression, though in the East

it is still extant—the room looked really
splendid, compared with the poor semp-
stress's. It was far more spacious than
any we had seen, and was in fact a double
room—the bed being about four feet
distant from the dinner-table. Odds and
ends of clothing lay scattered here and
there, amidst a chaos of cheap nicknacks
and some domestic crockery. The floor,
not overclean, was partly covered by some
carpet, and the walls, not over white, were
well-nigh wholly hidden by a lot of large
cheap pictures, and a number of small
photographs. "Plenty of colour for your
money," had very plainly been the maxim
of the purchaser, and viewed only from
this point, his buying had been fortunate.
One of these high-toned works of art
showed a clown in full stage costume, with
a six-feet string of sausages, giving a
dancing-lesson to a pretty little child, who,
attired as a fairy, was practising her steps.
Another biggish picture, more highly-
coloured still, with plenty of red about the
lips and cheeks, and black about the curly
hair and bushy beard, had been, not very
obviously, enlarged from father's photograph, which, for purpose of comparison,
was hanging close at hand. A little empty
cage was suspended from the ceiling, just
over the table. Noticing its emptiness, I
heard a piteous tale of how (the lamp
behaving badly in the absence of its
mistress) a poor little feathered prisoner
had, by sad mishap, been slowly smoked
to death.

There were likewise six brass candle-
sticks ranged upon the chimney-piece, and

these aroused my admiration more than all the works of art. "But they're dreadful dusty, an' want a polish badly," said the woman in apology for their neglected state. "They'll get it too, come Saturday," she added, as she caught my eye, just glancing at the chaos. "Yes, it's a rare mess as the room is in. But you know you can't be all'ys as you'd like to be. 'Speshly when you've got a lot o' little 'uns to look after, and your husbin's clothes to see to, and him a workin' in the coal too, it takes a sight o' washin' to make his shirt-sleeves clean."

The "husbin" worked at certain gas-works not far distant, whence he weekly brought his wife a sovereign for her house-keeping. "He earns more nor that, though," said the mother with a smile; "but he puts it away somewhere. No, it don't go down his throat now. He's a tee-tottler, is my husbin'. We're all teetottlers here, and he's the strictest of the lot. But he investes of it somewheres, in the post-orfice per'aps. 'Cause he's precious careful now he is, now as he've took the pledge. Says he, 'It's well to have a trifle 'andy like,' says he, 'case as you falls ill or gets a accident,' he says. For one can't all'ys be healthy, though he's a careful one, he is, and he don't go a runnin' of no risks as he can't help. But there, 'savin's better'n borryin',' that's what he says. An' mind you, he's about right there, he is. Borryin's a bad thing. When folks begin a borryin', they mostly ends a buryin'. Often drinks theirselves to death they does, 'cause they keeps gettin' deeper in, until they're right down desperate."

Only the lodger

"Many's the time I've bin a lyin' on the one side o' the gutter, & there was my own husbin a lyin' on the tother"

Face page 74.

The speaker, a Creole, was born at Havre, it appeared, though speaking English fluently, and with no trace of foreign accent. She looked strongly built enough to be the parent of ten children, her two firstborn being twin sons, aged now twenty-six. Six of her children still lived with her, five of whom were present, and all were dark and woolly-headed like herself. "They're a deal fonder o' him now," continued she reflectively, and then added with a laugh, "now as he don't wallup them. They used to catch it hot a' times, when he were in the drink. An' they're fonder o' me too, an' ain't so much afeerd o' me, now as I've reformed. Well there, I was a bad 'un, now weren't I, Mr. Austin? A blessed day it was, when your mission-chaps got hold o' me, that time I were so mad. An' a 'ardish work you had, too, when you first took me in 'and. Many's the time I've been a lying on the one side o' the gutter, an' there was my own husbin' a lying on the t'other, an' both of us so tight as we had to be picked out of it. I often wonder I'd not done for some o' them poor children, when I'd got the devil in me, through the drink. One time I rem'ber ketchin' up the bilin' kettle, and a chuckin' it bang at 'em, but it missed 'em by good luck."

I asked her if she recollected when it was her house was last put in repair; for it looked rather rickety, and seemed only lath and plaster. "Well, sir," she answered with a smile, "maybe my memory is bad, but I can't really reck'lect as anythin's been done since we've been here, and that's now

seven year come next August. And it
don't look over air-tight, do it, when you
come to see the cracks there is ? Nor it
wouldn't take a hearthquake to bring it on
our 'eads neither. But there, we somehow
makes it do, an' it keeps us fairish warm,
for there's a pretty tidy lot of us to live in
it. My boy Tom, he often says to me,
'Mother,' he says, 'I wonder why you likes
to live in that old pigsty.' But he've a
house of his own, has Tom, now as he've
got married, an' he seems proud about his
place too, 'cause, you see, his missus keeps a
little shop there. 'Why, you papers it,' he
says, 'and paintes it you does, and 'angs
your pictur's on the walls, an' there you
cosies yourself up, an' makes believe as you
live comfor'able. But it ain't much of a
'ouse for a family o' Christyuns. Why, my
old moke,' says he, 'would hardly like to
live in it.'

"Ah, you're a lookin' at that box, sir,"
continued my informant, whose tongue ran
on so glibly that possibly some slight im-
pediment in her speech might, when it
occurred, be welcomed by her family.
"Well, yes, it do seem a bit cur'ous.
That's a 'armonium, that's what it is, an'
plays The Bells of 'Eaven beautiful. My
husbin' bought it speshal for to give me
my last buthday. Cost him a sight o'
money. Two pun' seven an' six, it did;
true as ever I stan' here it did. Says he,
'Old woman, I've been thinkin' as your
voice is growin' a bit 'usky like. 'Tain't
so 'earty as it were, nor yet so strong for
singin' neither. So, as you're fond o'
music,' he says, 'I've bought you this

here hinstrument,' says he. 'Well, yes,' he says, 'it cost me a bit dear, an' it's kinder of a lux'ry. But since we've give the drink up, we can pretty well afford it.' So now, you know, he often plays a toon or two to amuse us in the evenin'; and sometimes of a Sunday, when he's a playin' of a 'im, we get a reg'lar congeregation out there in the court, we do."

TRAVELS IN THE EAST.

PART V.*

LEAVING the owner of the "'armonium" in her rickety old dwelling, with the expression of a hope that a sudden puff of wind—not to contemplate an earthquake—might not bring it tumbling down about her ears, we went upon our way through the wilds of the far East. A few minutes' brisk walking brought us to the foot of a little flight of stairs, which we proceeded to ascend for a dozen feet or so, until, on entering a small room, we found ourselves in presence of a neat little old lady, whose hair was nearly white, and who was sitting hard at work.

Everything about the chamber looked most scrupulously clean, forming a marked contrast to the house we had just left. Fully one half of the floor was covered by the bedstead, and a tiny strip of carpet was laid upon the rest. The bare boards, where revealed, appeared as though the scrubbing-brush were not a chance acquaintance, but a constant friend and visitor. Equally well scrubbed was the top of the

---

* ALL THE YEAR ROUND, March 29, 1884.

small table which stood beneath the window, and which, except the bedstead, and no fewer than seven chairs, was all the furniture displayed. The number of these chairs a little puzzled me at first, for I had learned that the only other dweller in the room was another neat old lady, who was out in quest of work. But overhearing a stage-whisper about certain "better days," and a husband who had charge of "fifteen hundred lamps" (whereof that of Aladdin, alas! had not been one), I concluded that the chairs were kept as relics of the past, and possibly at midnight were filled by a select society of ghosts.

A tiny fire was flickering in a tidily-kept grate—the spelling of the last word must be carefully attended to, for the adjective would be completely out of place. So very little heat was engendered by the process that the fire appeared to flicker merely for form's sake. The amount of coal expended at that slow rate of consumption could hardly have exceeded a farthing's-worth a day. A small kettle stood silent by the side of the small fire; indeed, thrice the heat emitted could have scarcely made it sing. In front, by way of hearthrug, lay a solemn-looking cat, who appeared, like his old mistress, to be saddened by the memory of departed better days. By way of decoration, he wore a bright brass collar, which had probably been saved when the fortunes of the family had been untimely wrecked. Excepting the worn wedding-ring adorning the old lady, the cat's collar was the only ornament or jewellery displayed in the

apartment, or upon the person of either of
its inmates.

"Ah," sighed the old lady, ".I wasn't
born like this, you know," and her statement, taken literally, must have been quite
true. "I've lived like a lady," she continued
rather sadly, "for I kept a servant once."
This she added as a proof of her ladylike
existence, and to show us what high altitude her rank had once attained. She still
kept up her old position in society, and
abstained from the word " sir " when she
addressed me or my guide. She claimed
plainly some distinction from the poor folk
who lived near her, at whom, indeed, I
fancy I detected a slight shadow of a sneer,
when I tried to compliment her on the
cleanness of her room. "Ah yes," she
replied with a smile of satisfaction, " you
see I've always been brought up to it.
When I kept my. servant I was always
used to seeing things kept nice, and clean,
and tidy. I could never live in a litter as
those poor people do, you know."

Those poor people ! Poor old lady !
And she, perhaps, among the poorest of
the poor, and daily working her old fingers
to the bone that she might live. But who
could smile at her small vanity, in the sight
of her sad poverty and the terrible priva-
tion which appeared so bravely borne ?
And who could help admiring her per-
severing cleanliness, and tidiness, and neat-
ness, in all the trial and the trouble of her
sorely fallen fortune and her sadly faded
life ? Surely, in despite of all the darkness
of her days, she had set a bright example
to some of " those poor people " who appear

"Ah! I wasn't born like this you know."

Face page 80.

to hold that poverty must be allied with dirt, and that they must be slovenly because they are not rich.

Fallen from her high estate, wherein she kept a servant, and had been mated to the keeper of fifteen hundred lamps—the provider of enlightenment, if not himself a brilliant man—the old lady, while she prattled, kept her needle briskly going, and her white hairs low bowed down over a coarse but clean blue shirt. Such garments it was now her fate to "finish," as she phrased it—a process which involved the cutting and the stitching of half-a-dozen button-holes, the sewing on of seven buttons, and the final stitching of a pair of flaps and cuffs. A farthing a shirt was all the wages she received; but even this was not all profit, for there had to be deducted the cost of the cotton, whereof a penny reel was barely sufficient for the finishing of four-and-twenty shirts. By working pretty hard for fourteen hours at a sitting, she could contrive to finish, say, two dozen in the day, and the rent she and her friend (who was a single lady still, and had likewise seen better days) were forced to pay for their small room, was just defrayed by finishing ten dozen every week. Thus the labour of five days of fourteen hours work apiece was entirely devoted to the sum due to the landlord, in so far as one of the two workers was concerned, and on her remnant of the work, and on the week's work of the other, the pair of poor old ladies were dependent for their clothing, and their firing, and their food.

There were three other small rooms in

the house which these old ladies had
honoured by their residence; and each of
these small rooms was separately tenanted,
and, indeed, might truly be regarded as a
home. All the occupants were absent,
excepting a stray child or so, too small to
seek for work; but a peep into their rooms
sufficed to prove that the old ladies were
unrivalled in possession of a clean and
tidy home.

Desirous of a contrast, I bethought me
of a dustman, whose home perhaps might
indicate his trade, and possibly show traces of
the dirt wherewith he dwelt. As a cobbler's
wife proverbially seldom goes well shod,
so a dustman's wife might rarely see her
room undimmed by dust. Moreover, I had
heard in my youth a comic story about a
dustman whose profession, I remember,
was made to rhyme with "fust man," to
whom—i.e., to Adam—his pedigree was
briefly, but ingeniously traced. By a
sudden freak of memory the refrain of
this old ditty flashed across my mind, and
I felt impelled to ask if there were dustmen in the neighbourhood, that I might
visit the abode of one, and make a mental
note of what was comical about it.

My wish was granted as readily as a
whim is in a fairy-tale. Without the aid
of any magical appliance for our transport,
such, for instance, as the moving-carpet of
Prince Ahmed, half-a-dozen minutes after
quitting the poor shirt-maker sufficed to
bring us to the dwelling whereof I was in
quest. It stood at the far end of a filthy
cul de sac, which formed a little outlet from
a rather narrow street; the beauty of whose

aspect was not rendered more attractive by a quantity of clothes'-lines, whereon were dangling sundry garments which hardly looked much cleaner for having been to the wash. One side of the court, which bore a royal title, comprised some six or seven extremely shabby tenements—they really seemed too small to be spoken of as houses—while in the middle of the other stood a rusty iron post, which proved, upon a nearer view, to be a dirty pump. This was flanked to right and left by sundry little squares of brickwork, whose chief purpose seemed to be the emission of bad smells. In some of these small out-buildings lay a little heap of cinders or a lump or two of coal; and in the corners there were gathered a few useless odds and ends, which might have well been shot as rubbish on the dust-heap that was near, although then hidden from our sight. As we were afterwards informed, all the dwellers in the court threw their dirt into one dust-bin; and this being used in common by two score or so of people, and very seldom emptied more than twice a month, perhaps it was no wonder that by following our noses we soon found out its whereabouts, and were able to acknowledge that it really seemed to focus all the foul smells of the court.

On the loose and broken tiles which formed the roof of these out-buildings, sat an evil-eyed, torn-eared, and mangy-looking cat. Pointing "the pleased oar," or, at any rate, its tatters, and wagging "the expectant tail," as well as could be wished in its abbreviated state, he looked wistfully at somebody, who probably was eating something, in a room which was just level with the roof whereon he sat. Presently this somebody, invisible to us, through a broken pane of glass pitched a small piece of potato, which with great alacrity was pounced on by poor puss. He instantly was joined by two other torn-eared cats, whose coats sadly wanted brushing, and whose general appearance showed a life much out of luck. Another morsel of potato being chucked out on the roof, there ensued forthwith the freest of free feline fights for its possession, and we were left to fancy what a battle would ensue were a pennyworth of cat's-meat thrown before the combatants, who clearly found it difficult in that poorly-feeding district to save themselves from starving by the few mice they could catch.

Of the Home of the Happy Dustman (happy because exempt by law from Sunday labour) a pretty picture might be made for a pious magazine; but I shall not attempt to draw upon my fancy for any such a work. The sketch I here present was made upon the spot, and though some few minor details may have escaped my notice, the points of special picturesqueness have been faithfully preserved. I abstain from highly colouring the plain pencilling I made, and from blackening the description by extra work with pen and ink.

The door of the house was open, and the door of the room likewise, which was on the ground-floor, there being one floor over it. This room—of ten feet square, say

The home of the happy dustman

Face page 84.

—formed the Happy Dustman's Home, and gave shelter to his wife and two young dustmen of the future, who at present were small boys. In the doorway stood a woman of about four or five and fifty, some-what frowsy and ill-favoured, who, although the doors were open, did not bid us come in. On the contrary, indeed, she did her best to keep us out, alleging as a reason that the place was "in a litter," which recalled me the literary dustman of the song. S likewise urged as her excuse that she was ": tidyin' up a bit," for her daughter was engaged in working at "the 'Eaps." We said politely that we were sorry for the absence of the lady; but that, though we were denied the pleasure of her company, we hoped we might enjoy the privilege of entrance to her room. This at length was granted with a grunt, which might have been mistaken for a negative reply to our request. But we construed the sound otherwise, and passed the threshold of the home, with a promise to make due excuse for its untidy state. "You see," said the old woman, "she lef' it in a litter, bein' a bit 'urried like for gettin' to the 'Eaps," and, indeed, throughout the conversation which ensued, continual hints were dropped about the litter being "temp'ry," and soon to be set right by the task of "tidying up."

Tidying up! Well, yes. It clearly was not quite a needless operation, te judge from the first glance. The confusion we had witnessed in the house of the good Creole was as order to the chaos which we discovered here. "A place for everything and everything in its place;" this was the

rule of life enjoined me in my youth, and
a vast saving of time this fine old-fashioned
maxim is certain, if adhered to, to foster
and induce. Here the rule of life observed
was precisely the reverse. "A place for
nothing, and nothing in its place." Such
seemed to have been the happy dustman's
happy thought, when asked what was his
notion of a motto for a household; and
considerable pains appeared to have been
taken in obeying its behest.

The dirty floor was partly hidden by
small scraps of dirty sacking, which chiefly
served to make the bare boards look more
bare. Dirty bits of sacking lay also on
the bedstead, and formed, indeed, the bed-
linen, for there were neither blanket, nor
counterpane, nor sheets. The substitutes
were anything but sightly to behold, as
they lay all heaped and huddled anyhow,
in what a tidy mistress would have termed
a "horrid mess." A limp bolster and lean
pillow lay also on the bed, and might, perhaps, have lately been picked out of a dust-
hole, so grimy was their look. Under the
unclean window stood a small deal table,
whereon a battered teapot and some unwashed cups and saucers, and some half-
munched crusts of bread, lay scattered all
about, and seemed as though they all had
met there by the merest accident, and were
not to be regarded in the light of mutual
friends. Huddled in one corner, as if half-
ashamed of taking so much room, and
being of so little use, stood a dingy chest
of drawers, with a couple of porcelain
poodles, hideous to behold, and some other
china ornaments, encumbering its dusty

top. Half-a-dozen wooden chairs, some with a fractured leg, and some with a broken back, were scattered here and there; one lay upside down, and another had apparently been used by way of toilet-table, for on its grimy seat there lay a scrap of soap, beside a partly toothless and a wholly unclean comb. For further purposes of toilet, a tub stood on the hearth, with a little dirty water in it; and near it was a bit of ragged linen which might once have been a towel, when it lived in better days. Before the empty fireplace stood a shabby, broken fender, and in the way of fire-irons it held an old bent poker, which I hoped had not been used as an instrument of torture, or a weapon of offence.

On the wall, by way of ornament, there hung an old Dutch clock, with a dirty pair of hands and an extremely filthy face. I say, by way of ornament, for it was clearly of no use. Both its hands were pointing idly to the figure VI, and to stir them into motion there were to be seen neither pendulum nor weights. "It ain't o' much account, or it wouldn't be a 'angin' there," remarked the old woman, with rather an air of mystery; but I own I failed to fathom the deep meaning of her words. For further mural decoration there were a pair of coloured prints—one, with a row of blooming, potted lilies and blazing, lighted candles, representing the " Interior of the Grave of the Holy Virgin," if we might believe the legend printed at the foot. The other, equally ill designed, though hardly so pretentious, depicted the

"Interior of the Grave of Christ." These
samples of high art were of foreign manufacture, and bore the name of "Lipschitz,"
in grateful recognition of their publisher's
great fame. They had been bought, said
the old woman, by the payment of a
shilling weekly for eleven weeks. Were
they put up for sale at Christie's—remote
as seems the likelihood of any such event
—it is doubtful if the bidding could by any
means be raised to one-eleventh part of the
price which they had cost.

Another tawdry print, coarsely coloured
like the pair, was hung on the wall opposite;
its title, "Ecce Homo," being, with the
printer's name, in foreign type. The room
further was embellished by a few more
cheap engravings, chiefly sacred in their
subject, and one coarse sporting print.
Something in the sight of these decorative
objects impelled me to enquire if their
owner were a Catholic, and as a denial was
given with some vehemence, I excused
myself by saying that the name of his
wife's mother had induced me to imagine
him Hibernian by birth. "Shure we're
Cockney-born, the hull of us," affirmed that
lady forcibly, but I am free to own that
there was something in her accent, as she
made the affirmation, which, if noticed in
a witness-box, might have been cited as a
reason for a doubt of her good faith.

The dustman was her son-in-law, she
proceeded to reiterate, and "a goodish sort
he was, too," she furthermore remarked.
He daily "arned two shillen, or it might be
'arf-a-crown," while his better half contrived,
if she were lucky, to gain eighteenpence a

day by labour previously described as "working at the 'Eaps." Dimly guessing what the "'Eaps" were, I shyly put a question which led to my enlightenment. "She siftes of the dust, shure, an' sortes of it out, for there's stuff in it may be as is wuth the pickin' over, and a sellin' to the Stores." I presumed she meant the stores where the Black Doll is suspended, as a sign to attract custom. Few other stores, I fancy, would deal much in the merchandise exported from the 'Eaps.

"Walables? 'Taint likely. Shure the sarvants picks 'em out afore they gits into the dust 'ole. There ain't a blessed bone as the cook don't get a 'old on. Waste? Yis shure, she'd heard there was a sight o' waste a' times, down in the kitchen of the swells." But she did not somehow notice the crusts of bread-and-butter which lay scattered on the table, and which would probably be thrown into the dust-bin in the course of her "tidying up."

The rent of this one room was two and threepence weekly, the landlord "doing" the repairs, and the tenants too, perhaps. There were large cracks in the walls, which looked as though they were fast losing the only coat of whitewash which ever had been theirs. The little paint there was had nearly disappeared beneath the dirt that covered it. A window-pane was broken, and stuffed up with some paper, and the plaster in big patches was peeling from the ceiling, and bits of it were lying on the bed and on the floor. "Shure an' it'll be tumblin' on the boys, and crackin' of their skulls when they're aslape," said their old grandmother, her brogue getting the better of her as she poured some of the vials of her wrath upon the landlord, with whom she plainly had a feud.

On my noticing the dust-bin, just opposite the door, and remarking that it hardly could be deemed a wholesome neighbour, judging by its smell, she replied, "Deed, it tain't so bad jist now. Shure 'tis in summer you should smell it." And then her anger blazed forth at the misdeeds of the neighbours—nine families there were of them—who misused their common property, and mistook the pavement for the dust-bin of the court. "They throws their stuff down anywheres a'most," she plaintively complained. "They do make me so aggarawated. 'Pon me sowl, they scatters it about for all the world like sowing seed."

We paid one or two more visits before we left the court, to which I may perhaps find reason to return. In the West, as in the East, one may be easily presented at such a court as this, and doubtless many an honest home may be discovered even dirtier than the one I have described. There may be nothing very singular in the sketch which I have drawn, and maybe many of my readers may know where a companion picture might be made. Poverty may make a man acquainted with queer bedding as well as with strange bedfellows, and there is no reason why honesty should never dwell divorced from cleanliness of life. Still, unless upon the principle that the driver of fat oxen should himself be fat, I was puzzled to make out why the dustman's home I saw was so conspicuous for dirt. Whether any drop of Irish blood were flowing in the veins of the family who lived in it, or, if so, whether such a fact was sufficient to account for the filthiness we found—these are problems which are far too deep for my philosophy to fathom, and which the reader will excuse me from endeavouring to solve.

TRAVELS IN THE EAST.

PART VI.*

"AND now," said I, on quitting the
mother of the dustman's wife, engaged
upon her Sisyphean task of tidying up;
"and now I want to see the home of one
of the poor matchbox-makers, for I have
heard they are the worst paid of all the
very ill-paid workers in the East."

"Have then thy wish!" my guide
might have replied, had he been given to
quote poetry. But being more business-
like, he simply said: "All right;" and
without leaving the court where the dustman had his home, we found the other
home whereof I was in quest.

The room was on the ground, and was
of the same smallness—I can hardly call it
size—as most of the apartments, or dwellings, one may term them, we had previously seen. The walls were full of
cracks and blotches bare of plaster. What
their colour once had been it was not easy
to determine, for all their surface was
absorbed by a prevailing hue of dirt. The
ceiling, too, seemed mostly made to match
the walls both in regard to falling plaster

---

* ALL THE YEAR ROUND, April 5, 1884.

and all-pervading griminess, and dinginess,
and dust. The bare floor was half-covered
by a worn-out wooden bedstead, which, in
the way of bed, had nothing but the sacking stretched across whereon the mattress
should have lain; together with a little
hay or straw, or fodder of some sort—it
was certainly not feathers—stuffed limply
into what might once have held potatoes,
but was far too shrunk and meagre in
dimension to be likened to Jack Falstaff's
"intolerable quantity of sack."

A widowed knife without a fork; a
wedded pair of teaspoons, as different in
size as many married couples, but bearing
each a sadly worn and battered look; a
brace or two of cups, estranged from their
own saucers and mated to others which
did not appear to match; some half-a-
dozen plates, that were generally cracked;
and a teapot which was leading a terribly
loose life, in so far as touched its handle
and its lid—these were the only signs,
visible and outward, of anything like eating or sitting down to meals. Sitting
down, indeed, would have been a little
difficult, except in Turkish fashion by
squatting on the floor, for there were only
a couple of chairs, and one was serving as
a work-stool, and was covered with paste
and paper, while the other seemed an in-
valid, and was propped against the wall,
as though weak in the legs or injured in
the back.

By the door stood a small table with
strips of thin wood ranged upon it,
together with a pair of very venerable
scissors, and more paper, and more paste.

Beside a tiny fire there stood a little pile of
boxes, made for holding night-lights, which
were doing their very best to be dried by
the small heat. Near them sat erect, as
though a sentinel on guard, a sharp-eyed,
grey - and - white, suspicious - looking cat.
Except, perhaps, the paste-pot, which was
valuable for business, there was little household property worth the care to watch.
But pussy kept her eye on us, as though
prepared to make a pounce, like a policeman on a burglar, if she detected the least
symptoms of nefarious design.

On a shelf by the chimney lay a bit or
two of crockery, made less for use than
ornament, and of little use for that.
Conspicuous in the centre, and kept doubtless as a relic of departed days of comfort, stood a large two-handled mug of not
quite modern make. A dealer might have
bought it for a shilling at a sale, or possibly
for sixpence if sold by private contract,
and very likely afterwards have labelled it
"Old Staffordshire," and have allowed
some young collector to acquire it as "a
bargain," say, for half-a-guinea, or failing
the collector, have eventually sold it, in a
spasm of generosity, for the sum of three
half-crowns. The only other sign of
luxury, departed from the dwelling with
departed better times, was apparent in a
leash of tiny little cages, suspended near
the ceiling, which was hardly more than
six feet from the floor. There was, however, nothing moving in these small
Bastilles. The little prisoners had all
been sold, and perhaps it was as well for
them, or else they might have starved.

While we were surveying this sad scene
of desolation, its mistress returned suddenly, and gave a feeble echo, being somewhat out of breath, to the greeting of my
guide. She was very thinly clothed, but
with some slight show of mourning. · On
her head she wore a something which
might once have been a bonnet, but could
hardly make pretence of having kept its
normal shape. Her face was very pale,
and her hands were thin and shaking, and,
as she spoke, there seemed to be a shiver
·in her voice. Wrapped under her old
shawl she carried a small bottle, to fetch
which, she told us, she had been to the
hospital. She was an out-patient, for her
cough was very bad. It was " shaking the
life out of her," she quiveringly declared.

Pitiably sad was the story of her life,
and her present way of living—or shall I
say of dying? After every dozen words or
so she paused to gasp for breath, and held
her hand pressed to her side, as if in
frequent pangs of pain. She had been
left a widow less than fifteen months ago;
her husband, a dock-labourer, having died
in the infirmary at Bromley; and her
grown-up son and daughter, who were
living with her then, had been living with
her since. The son pursued the same profession as his father, and found it full of
workers and not so full of work. To help
to pay the rent (which for their one room
was two and threepence weekly), and to
buy such food and clothing as the son
failed to provide, the daughter with her
mother worked at making match-boxes, or,
when she got a chance, sold watercress or

flowers, which she was doing when we called.

The poor widow confessed that the match-box manufacture was not a paying trade. The poor people who worked at it were rewarded for their labour at the rate of twopence-farthing for each completed gross. That was the gross price, if I may venture so to term it; but the net amount received was actually less. Taskmasters of old had declined providing straw for the poor who slaved at brickmaking, and merchants nowadays demanded of the poor who made their match-boxes that they should provide the paste. The cost of the materials was little, it was true, but time was wasted in the making, and time was rather precious when counted in the price. Fire too was required both for the making of the paste and for the drying of the boxes after they were made. But, these drawbacks notwithstanding, twopence-farthing for twelve dozen was the liberal rate of payment, and on the same scale of munificence was the wage for making night-light boxes, although upon the whole the work was rather harder, the boxes being longer and being made with lids.

I enquired of what disease it was her husband died. "Same as I'm a-doing—Starvation," she replied a little grimly, with a gasp that added emphasis to the plainness of her speech. "I've had no food since Sunday," she proceeded to observe; and, mind, it was on Wednesday that we heard the observation. Being a little startled, I questioned her more closely. Perhaps her memory was faulty, or perhaps

The match-box maker:

Face page 96.

she tried to make the worst of her sad plight. But all she could remember was a cup or two of tea—the last pinch they had left—and a morsel of dry bread scarce big enough to bite.

"And we've sold everything we've got a'most. Excep' the bed we're lying on. And there ain't much o' that. Not as many 'ud care to buy. But there, God's good, they say. He'll help us yet maybe. I trust in Him, I do. But I'm a'most past His help."

All this was said in gasps, with a dry cough now and then, that well-nigh choked her utterance; and with a quiver in her figure and a quaver in her voice. If she were acting, as Mr. Bumble might suggest, she certainly bade fair to shine upon the stage, and might "star" it in the provinces with great prospect of success.

I questioned her about her husband, and the causes of his illness.

"He worked mostly at the docks," she said, "and we got on pretty comfor'able. But there come a baddish time, an' he couldn't get no work sca'ce, an' he got weak for want o' food. An' then he catched a chill a waitin' in the wet. So he went to the infirney, an' lay there till he died. Day arter Christmas Day—merry Christmas as they calls it. We wasn't very merry with him there lying dead, and we'd nothin' much to eat."

From further information, elicited in gasps, I learned some ghastly details as to the death which had occurred, and the days that had elapsed before the funeral took place. The body, it appeared, had been sent home in a "shell," for the widow wished, if possible, to avoid a parish burial, having perhaps heard of the grim chorus of the song :

Rattle his bones
Over the stones,
He's only a pauper whom nobody owns.

So her son got up a "Lead" (pronounced to rhyme with "need"), which, as she explained, was a meeting of their friends and neighbours, who were privately invited to subscribe towards a private burial. They, however, were so poor that only forty shillings was, in pennies and in sixpences, collected at the "Lead," and this being less than half the undertaker's lowest charge, she was reluctantly compelled, after fifteen days of waiting, to seek for parish help.

"But," I could not resist enquiring, "did he—did the shell remain here all this while?"

"Yes," replied the widow, gasping as before. "It stood here upon trestles, just where you're a stan'in', an' me an' my daughter slep' beside it on the bed, and her brother slep' beside it down there on the floor. No, we never saw no doctor, nor no Sanitaray 'Spectre, nor we didn't want to. They all'ys make a fuss, an' quarrels, too, like cats. Leastways so they say. But I don't know much about 'em, though I don't think they're much good."

To change this painful subject, I pointed to the plaster which was peeling from the walls, and falling from the ceiling, and I asked her when she thought the landlord would repair the room.

"Haven't got no landlord," was the

answer. "She's a lady. Leastways so they calls her. She's a 'ard 'un, she is. Lives down in the Dog Road, nigh to The Blind Beggar. Yes, that's a public-'ouse. Reg'lar 'ard 'un, she is. Told me on'y yest'day if rent worn't paid to-morrer she'd put my things out in the street. An' God knows how I'm to pay it, if my son don't get a job."

She said this, not complainingly, but as though stating a plain fact. There was no covert appeal to us for charity, nor sly glance to see if we were moved by her sad story; that sharp but furtive look which a beggar by profession often finds a useful guide in framing his next speech. Mr. Ebenezer Scrooge, before the hour of his conversion, might have sworn that she was shamming, and have buttoned up his pockets in a fit of righteous wrath at her manifest imposture and mendicant attempt. But after seeing the three Spirits, Mr. Scrooge, if he had listened while the widow told her story, would no doubt have done as I did, and relieved her of the fear of being turned into the street.

Just as the poor widow was ending her sad story, and with trembling hands had resumed her ill-paid work, we were cheered by the arrival of a sturdy little girl, with bright brown eyes, and hair all towzled by the wind, and some out-door-grown and healthy-looking roses on her cheeks. She wore a very shabby dress, but had good thick shoes to her feet. Brisk in manner, if not brusque, and speaking in short sentences, she seemed as if she had much business on her hands, and her voice, like her hair, was roughened, as it were, by exposure in the streets.

She had been out selling a few "creeses," she informed us, and had now returned to look after the children, and to finish washing a few "things" of theirs, and some of her papa's. But for her mentioning the children in this maternal manner, I might have foolishly mistaken her for being one of them herself. My guide, however, with due deference, addressed her as "Little Mother," which she apparently accepted as her rightful title. Being delicately questioned on the subject of her age, she owned to being sixteen, but confessed the age was counted from her birthday in next August, for young ladies love to reckon a few months in advance.

As I wished to hear a little of her ways and means of life, she invited me politely, albeit a little gruffly, to visit her at home. So we bade adieu to the poor widow, and followed Little Mother up some steep and narrow stairs, to the unusual altitude of an Eastern second floor. Entering a low doorway, we stood in a small room of barely seven feet in height. This chamber formed the home of Little Mother and three children and their father, whose wife, we learned, had died in "the dark days before Christmas" last, which certainly had not been brightened by her death. Father was nursing baby during Little Mother's absence, a poor, pale, sad-eyed baby, wrapped in an old threadbare shawl, and carried tenderly in his arms with never a whine nor whimper, the while father walked about.

Master Suckthumb

"Little mother -"

Squatting on the floor was a white-faced little boy, half dressed in a blue jersey, with patches in the sleeves, which scarcely reached below the elbow. He wore, likewise, some blue " small clothes," which were worthy of their name, for they reached hardly to the knee, and showed a longish bit of bare leg over a bare foot. In the absence of a lollipop or piece of barley-sugar, he was employed in sucking his thumb with amazing perseverance. I asked him what his name was, and his father answered "Henry," the boy having his mouth too full of thumb to make an audible reply.

Father was clean-shaven and tidy in his appearance, though he had not much to boast of in the matter of attire. He spoke very civilly, in rather a weak voice, and his cheeks bore out the notion of his being underfed. He was a costermonger by profession, but wasn't no ways pertickler. Go anywheres he would, and do anything a'most, if so be as he could earn an honest penny by his work. To-day he'd been acrost the river to the Commercial Docks, having heerd there, were a ship in, and a prospec' of a job. But bless him, though he got there afore six, there was scores of 'em a-waiting; and after all it worn't no go, 'cause the ship hadn't come in yet. And that was about the way of it, 'most everywheres it was. " If there's ever such a little bit o' work a-wantin' to be done, there's hunderds of 'em flocks to it. And it's 'ard lines on a chap as have got his mouth to fill, and four little uns beside, too. Not so very little neither, leastways some of them there mouths ain't." This

he added with a smile as he looked at
Little Mother, who, however, was too busy
at her wash-tub to notice the small sarcasm
her papa cast in her teeth.

Two shillings and threepence a week was
the rent of his small room, which was
higher from the ground and lower in its
ceiling than any I had seen. Some floor-
boards were loose, and when trodden on
abruptly seemed to threaten a descent into
the chamber underneath. There was not
a scrap of carpet to hide any defects, nor
were there any photographs or cheap
pictures on the walls to conceal their want
of paint. There was a wooden bedstead,
with the usual Eastern bedding of some
huddled bits of sacking; and there were a
table and a chair or two, with a stool,
whereon the wash-tub was conspicuously
placed. A large stain on the ceiling betrayed
a leaky roof, and in the small window I
saw two broken panes.

"They're Master Suckthumb's doing,"
said his father in apology. "He's to blame
for them there breakages, he is. Broke
'em with his ball, he did. He were a'most
all'ys a chuckin' it about whensoever me
an' Molly worn't upon the watch. If they's
left ever to theirselves, boys is all'ys up to
mischief. And one must leave 'em a while
when one's got to arn some grub for 'em.
You can't well be at home an' be out, too,
that's for sartin."

"Well, yes," cried I, correcting him,
"you may be at home, you know, and yet
be out of temper. But I think you're too
good-humoured to be ever out of that,"
I added with a smile, for indeed he looked

the picture of contentment and good-
nature, as he briskly walked about with
the baby in his arms. He seemed to relish
my small joke, and gave a little laugh as
he repeated it to Little Mother at the tub.
She was far too busy to indulge in idle
laughter, but she deigned to listen gravely,
and appeared to comprehend the purport
of the jest.

Enquiry being put why father had not
gone to morning-service for many Sundays
past—"Why, how can I?" he replied,
"when I haven't got no coat. I've on'y
this old jacket, which it ain't fit to be seen
in, special of a Sunday. I'd be willin'
enough to come, but I'd like to look
respectable. An' with them little uns to
feed, I really can't afford it. Beside,
there's baby to be nussed, an' he's gittin' a
bit 'eavyish, an' Molly can't be all'ys
mindin' him, you know. So I has to take
my turn at it; an' Molly works so 'ard o'
week days, she ought to rest a bit o'
Sunday. Why, when she's a sellin' creeses,
she must be early at the market, an' that's
nigh Obun way, you know, an' a tidy
tramp from 'ere that is. She've to get
there afore five, an' some mornin's afore
four, an' she'll 'ave to be afoot a' times
till six or seven a' night, if so be she ain't
no luck. But it's a goodish trade is creeses.
When I finds I've 'arf-a-crownd as I can
spare her for a spec, she'll make it nigh
to double by investin' it in creeses."

The conversation taking a commercial
turn, I was able to acquire some further
knowledge of the match trade. Little
Mother had worked at it, for lack of better

labour; and had not merely made the boxes, but had filled them with their matches—first, with a fixed knife, cutting all of these to fit. For this two-fold operation she had received, upon the average, threepence, or it might be, threepence-farthing, for four dozen boxes filled. "Starting work at seven punctual," as her father phrased it, and working pretty reg'lar till nigh on eight at night, she had contrived to earn as much as four shillings a week. She had even heard of workers who could weekly earn a crown; but they must keep tightish at it, and be most uncommon handy with their fingers, she opined, and not given much to gab.

Little Mother condescending to join us in our talk, I put a shilling in her hand, just wet out of the wash-tub, and asked if she could read what was impressed upon the coin. She frankly answered, "No," for she had "never gone to school. Never had the time," she added with some briskness, to which her father by a nod in silence signified assent. She knowed it were a shilling though, she proceeded to observe, and she knowed how many bundles of creeses she could buy with it, and how much she could sell 'em for, if she had any luck. She seemed sadly posed, however, when I propounded the old problem which had puzzled me in youth; anent the herring and a half that could be bought for just threehalfpence, and the number left indefinite to be purchased for elevenpence; the terms of buying being similar in either case of sale. Reduction being made in the estimate demanded, at length, by rather slow degrees, her father prompting audibly, she succeeded in stating a solution of the problem ; and she seemed very much relieved when, at my suggestion, she had pocketed the shilling which had caused such needless trouble to her mind.

I shook hands with Little Mother on wishing her farewell, and a good issue of her wash. I was likewise honoured with a shake by Master Suckthumb, who by a superhuman effort had succeeded in extracting his digit from his lips. He seemed rather in low spirits ; possibly from taking thought about the broken window, which his father had recalled to him ; or about the ball which he had lost in consequence of that lamented fracture, and which in his dearth of things to play with was doubtless a sad loss. He cheered up a little when I produced a penny, and suggested that perhaps he might buy another ball with it. But paternal wisdom hinted that another pane might suffer ; and so a peg-top was proposed and cheerfully accepted, on condition that the pegging should be done on the pavement of the court.

Another half-mile walk, and half-hour's visit at the end of it, both of which I may, perhaps, describe hereafter, brought to a conclusion my second Eastern travel ; which, on the whole, had saddened me more than the first. Again I entered the Cathedral, in my tramp through the City, and found the white-robed little choir-boys busied in their Lenten service, and musically chanting in a plaintive minor key. In the pauses of their singing the roar of the street traffic beat upon the ear, and re-

called me to the scenes of life and labour I
had left. How peaceful seemed that haven,
where all sat at their ease, and where no
signs were visible of misery and want!
And then there came the thought that the
poor were "always with us," though the
want of decent clothing might keep them
out of church. And there came, too, the
remembrance, reverential and refreshing,
that the finest of all sermons was preached
chiefly to the poor: who, with the promise
of a share in the kingdom of heaven, were
rightly and divinely accounted to be blessed.

TRAVELS IN THE EAST.

PART VII.*

WHEN I first projected my travels in
the East, I had no idea that I should go
as far as China, nor had I any notion that
a knowledge of Chinese would be useful in
my journey. Well, though I have not been
to China, I have visited a house where a
Chinaman is living; and though I found
him conversational, as far as his imperfect
English would permit, I might have gained
more information, if I had been able to
talk in his own language.

We found Jack Chinaman's abode in a
shabby little court, reached by a narrow
passage from a shabby little street, within
well-nigh a sling's throw of the Shadwell
railway-station. Setting forth from Stepney,
with my guide, soon after noon upon bright
St. Patrick's Day, a pennyworth of travelling had brought me down to Shadwell;
for, though Great in name, the railway
condescends to take small fares, and to
suit the little incomes of the poor folk in
its neighbourhood.

There was nothing New about the court
except its name, and there was nothing
new at all, not even in her name, about the

---

* ALL THE YEAR ROUND, April 12, 1884.

woman who there greeted us. Old and haggard in her looks, and, through effect of evil living, plainly looking older than her actual years would warrant, she wore a shabby bonnet that well-matched the shabby court, and a dress which in antiquity appeared to match herself. Her hands were skinny claws, crooked as with habit of holding in their clutch a gin-glass, let us say, or something of the sort. There seemed a palsy in their shaking, as she drew her ragged shawl about her scraggy throat. Her eyes were blear and blood-shot, and their lids were raw and red; and these, with sundry pimples and some blotches here and there, were the only show of colour in her pale and pasty face.

This lady, although English, was the wife of the Jack Chinaman whom we had come to visit, and who was really the Jack Chinaman described as not endowed with "the true secret of mixing," by the opium-smoking hag who kept the den described in "Edwin Drood." The court where we were standing might very well have been the original, in fact, of the "miserable court" where Mr. Jasper, on awaking from his narcotic trance, mistook the spike upon the bedpost for his cathedral spire.

Viewed from the outside, there was nothing in the aspect of the house from which the lady was emerging, to indicate connection with the Celestial Empire, or in any way to hint to us that a native of that empire was resident therein. It looked as small, and mean, and shabby as any of its neighbours; having a room on the ground-floor, and one on the floor above. The

lady acting as our pilot, we ascended to
this latter by the help of a small staircase
leading, with no passage, direct from the
front door. At a glance I guessed the
room to measure ten feet, say, by twelve,
and barely more than seven in height.
There was a sickly smell about it, even
now when nearly empty; but when a score
or so of smokers had slept there for some
hours, the wonder seemed to be that they
were not all choked.

By the door was a small fireplace, and
in front a small, bent fender, but no poker
and no tongs. Perhaps the fire-irons were
removed, like the knife of the Lascar who
slept by Mr. Jasper; being looked upon as
weapons of possible offence. There was a
small window just opposite the fireplace,
serving as much for ventilation—through
a cracked and dirty pane or two—as it
could do for light. The ceiling had been
yellow-washed, apparently, not long since,
and splashes of the colour were scattered
on the walls, which had once been painted
blue, as a contrasting tint. The room was
further beautified by a clothes-line stretched
across it, which seemed handy for a strang-
ling if any dreamer, on awaking from his
vision, felt that way inclined.

The floor of the chamber was carpetless
but clean, all traces of the night's work
having been removed. By way of furniture there were a couple of wooden chairs
and a brace of wooden bedsteads, placed
lengthways from the window, with a yard
of space between them. Each had a lame
leg which was supported by a brickbat;
and each had a low headboard, and like-

wise a low footboard, but no post with any spike. On each bedstead lay a mattress, rather hard and thin, but no bolster or pillow, and in lieu of sheets or counterpane, each was covered with some matting, either Indian or Chinese.

On the bed next to the door reclined the master of this mansion of opium-begotten bliss. He wore an English suit of clothes, at least it might have been a suit, if the rough grey vest had only matched the coat and trousers, which were made of smooth black cloth. They all three looked too large for him, as though picked up second-hand, or presented by some clients who found themselves too poor to pay for a good smoke. He had a cloth cap on his head, but had sacrificed his pigtail, and in lieu of it was growing a sparse and straggling little beard, or rather tuft, on his lean chin. His eyes were small, and sunken, and shaped in Chinese fashion, and his cheeks were sallow, thin, and hollow, as though from constant exercise of puffing at a pipe.

His wife, having introduced us, left to do some shopping; I might have thought some gin-shopping, if on her departure my guide had not informed me that such was not her practice, since she had signed the pledge. So, for half an hour or so, we had Jack Chinaman to talk to, and to listen to moreover, and none to overhear. The dreamings of an opium-taker, as given by De Quincey, are interesting, no doubt; but I fancy that Jack Chinaman could tell a tale or two about the dreamers of such dreams, which would afford some startling

Mr Earl and Young Dry.

Face page 110.

reading, if only he could somehow be brought truly to confess.

He spoke in a soft voice, but not very distinctly, and with somewhat of a drawl; and though he used no pigeon-English, it was frequently not easy to make out what he meant. He said his name was Ah See, at least such was the sound of it, as I pencilled it in English, not knowing how correctly to spell it in Chinese. But though Ah See was his name, he was commonly called Johnson, and indeed had grown so famous that the court wherein he lived was known as Johnson's Court.

"I sixty-two," he answered to a question of his age. "I come London forty-five ye-ar. Come as cook abo-ward ship that time. Go home some ye-ar after. Live he-ar twenty-nine ye-ar. In this ho-ouse. Yes. Mr. Dic-kens come see me one ni-ight. No, I not know him at a-all. Sergeant tell me—that Mr. Cha-arles Dic-kens. Sergeant a poli-ice, ye-es. I pre-etty well off then. Plenty ship in do-ocks. Ha-ave taken some time five pound, some-time ten pound in a we-ek. Sa-ave it, O yes. Put by plenty money then. Wi-ife fi-ind where I ke-ep it. Messed it all awa-ay in dri-ink. Wi-ife pretty ba-ad then. Gave her good sha-awl came from for-eign. Was soon put awa-ay. Ye-es, that's it, paw-awned for drink."

Here an interlude occurred, wherein there was much indistinct complaint, chiefly of the "wi-ife," and her misdeeds and drunkenness, which had been his ruin, until she had reformed. Now that the pledge was taken, she contrived somehow to keep it; and so domestic troubles were on the decrease. But he was sadly depressed by the badness of the times.

"Nothing came in last two ye-ar," complained he mournfully. "Thi-ink I have to go, so-oon. Can't stop he-ar much. Things very bad he-ar now. Had plenty lodgings once. All over the co-ourt. Now only this one ro-om for seboke."

This queer word puzzled me a while; but hearing it repeated, I soon learned by the context that it was simply meant for "smoke." A couple of opium-pipes lay beside him on the bed; bits of bamboo two feet long they were; one end being plugged up with a little piece of ivory, and the other, with no mouthpiece, being smoothed to touch the lips. Near the plugged end was the bowl of coarse and clumsy earthenware, coloured green, and having a small hollow, wherein was placed a little bit of opium, about as big as a large pea. The pipe appeared to need much puffing at to keep the drug alight, and much careful cleaning out of pitchy-looking ashes before it was refilled. And the pea had to be moulded and melted into shape upon the point of a long needle, in the flame of a small lamp, before it reached the proper state for putting in the pipe. When, after all the care and labour of preparing it and keeping it alight, it seemed merely to afford some half-a-score of whiffs.

In the half-hour that we spent with him, Mr. Ah See—alias Johnson—prepared, and filled, and smoked no fewer than four pipes. And in the intervals between them, he rolled and smoked three strongish cut-tobacco cigarettes. On my asking at what age he began the baleful practice, "I seboke now forty-two ye-ar," he replied, without an instant's hesitation, as though his memory were prompt. "Began at seven-tee-een. Was ve-ry ba-ad then. Brought up plenty bloo-ood. Doctor said I must seboke. So I try seboke. Bloo-ood stop and I get well. So I seboke ever si-ince. Hundred pipe a da-ay sometime. Ne-ver make me slee-eep now. Some ta-ake p'raps four, p'raps fi-ive. Then they slee-eep sound enough. They get sha-aky too. O yes, plenty sha-ake. My ha-and not sha-aky—see."

No, sure enough. It was lean, and even skinny, but, the while he held it forth, it showed no shiver of a shake. And though his age was over sixty, he had hardly a grey hair, and seemed hale and hearty, and fit enough for work, excepting that his right arm was rendered nearly useless, having, he alleged, been broken in his sleep. He had somehow doubled it beneath him, and cracked the bone close to the elbow, while dreaming, perhaps, that he was wrestling with a demon, engendered by the drug which is so devilish in its work.

Yet, if there were a question which of this worthy couple, Mr. Johnson and his wife, had most suffered by indulgence—the one taking to the drug, and the other to the drink—the lady's pallid face and well-nigh palsied fingers would show that greater harm and deadlier had been done by the drink.

We found a tidy little room downstairs,

when we had left the den where so many
dreams of cloudland had passed away in
smoke. It was clear that Mr. Ah See
could attend to creature comforts when
not engaged in business. When we walked
into his parlour, it looked clean, and even
pretty—in comparison, at least, with the
dreaming-room above. Somehow my
thoughts wandered to the parlour of the
spider, and its neat and trim appearance,
which, alas! had proved so fatally attractive
to the poor, weak-minded, and deluded fly.

The two angels who slept in this cleanly
little chamber had placed their bed close
to the casement, which was curtained with
white muslin, and showed no sign of being
cracked. The bed was fairly broad, view-
ing the smallness of the room, and boasted
of a bluish counterpane and a whitish pair
of sheets. There were some pictures on
the walls, of modern English manufacture,
but there was no specimen, either ancient
or modern, of any Chinese artist; not
even so much as a real china teapot or a
willow-pattern plate. The largest of the
pictures was a highly-coloured portrait of
Little Red Riding-hood, whereof the subject certainly was not to be mistaken,
though I doubted if Jack Chinaman were
familiar with the tale. There was a mirror
by the mantelpiece, the frame covered up
with paper, cut in parti-coloured strips—
less, perhaps, for art's sake than to keep it
from the flies. There likewise was a clock,
which, unlike most Eastern clocks, seemed
capable of going, for it actually ticked.
There was also a round table, sufficiently
expansive for a social festive purpose, and

strong enough to bear a joint of Christmas
beef. There was nothing on it now, however, but a stuffed canary, which the
Chinaman affirmed to have lived with him
"more than fifteen ye-ar," together with
some crockery, some for use and some for
ornament, but all of it of English, and not
Oriental make.

Altogether, it seemed likely that, despite
of his complaints about the badness of the
times, Mr. Ah See—alias Johnson—somehow still contrived to do a goodish bit of
business in his opium-smoking den, albeit
he declared that a shilling's-worth of his
"seboke-ing" mixture was sufficient for the
filling of four-and-twenty pipes. He claimed
to have turned Christian, as a solace to
his soul in his declining years, and possibly
as penance for the folly and the vices of
his manhood and his youth. "I great
rogue once. I very much bad then. I
quite alter now;" and he pointed, as he
spoke, to a couple of framed texts which
he had placed upon the wall, as if to prove
the fact of his conversion and his faith.

How far in his heart he may be now less
heathen than he was, it might be difficult
to gauge, though easier to guess. But the
truth is pretty certain that some ugly
tales are extant, of sailors lured, and
drugged, and robbed, and found at last
half-dead, having first of all, as a prelude
to this sequel, simply been half-drunk.
Mr. Ah See has, of course, no recollection
of these stories, which probably have sprung
from the invention of an enemy, and might
be told to the marines, or by the wags of
Tiger Bay. But it is possible that Mr.

Ah See may find it worth his while to close his tempting little den, if he lays claim to be a Christian, real and sincere; and if he would fain win sympathy, not to speak of some stray shillings, or even sovereigns, it may be, which for so interesting a convert might by certain weak-kneed people be most piously subscribed.

As a contrast to this gentleman and his luxury of living—at any rate so far as his cigarettes unlimited, and scores of opium-pipes a day—I will try to give an inkling, or it may be a pen-and-inkling, of a visit which I paid in my second day of travel, to the home of a poor widow; whom the converted Chinaman might copy with some profit, in so far as uncomplaining self-denial is concerned.

By the side of a thronged thoroughfare, just opposite a church, which, alas! is seldom crowded, we discovered a small shed built on a little scrap of ground, which really seemed too small to be accounted as a "Place." The shed at a rough guess was a dozen feet in length, and varied in its width from three feet six inches at one end to eight feet at the other. One of its long walls was of brick-work, and the other was of planks, and these in many places were an inch or so apart. The corners of the Place abutting on the thoroughfare, were occupied conspicuously on the one side by a coffee-palace, which had retired from competition; and on the other by a gin-palace, which certainly appeared to do a thriving trade. Seen by the roadside, near to a village or a farm, the shed might have been deemed to

Mr Ah See

Face page 116.

be a stable or a cow-house. Here, in this great city and bright centre of civilisation, it was humanly inhabited and dwelt in as a home.

Opening the door, without the prelude of a knock, we were welcomed very warmly by a pleasant little woman, about fifty years of age, business-like in manner, and extremely brisk in speech. She was very poorly clothed—indeed, her dress looked well-nigh threadbare; but in clothing and in person she was scrupulously clean. The house, or shed, or room, was as cleanly as herself, and seemed really almost comfortable—although the ceiling was patched up, and one window would not shut, and the plaster was in places peeling from the walls, and the shrunk door let the draught in, and the floor near to the corners showed many a little hole, and there was a rather large hole in the roof.

"Yes, it do want doing up a bit," observed the woman with a smile, as I noted these defects. "But there, we're happy enough in it," she added with another; "though it might be a bit higher;" this, after a moment, was spoken in apology, for at the point where I was standing, my bare head touched the ceiling. "But there, it's nothing when you're used to it," she proceeded to remark; and perceiving very possibly that she had found a willing listener, she continued with small ceasing in her fluent flow of speech. "Yes, it's low, there's no denyin'; but it's all the warmer. And one don't want no ladders when one wants to clean the ceiling, which I papered it myself I did, true as you stand there, I did, an' went an' bought the paper, an' made the paste myself. And me an' my son helpin' me, we both of us set to one day, an' somehow or another we mended of the roof, we did. 'Cause it used to leak most terrible, speshly when so be it blowed a bittish 'eavy. I dunno how we done it hardly, but the wet don't henter now not much, leastways excep' it's snowing, an' there's nothin' can't keep snow out when it come to melt, there ain't. An' it henters through the walls, too, though per'aps you'd hardly think it."

Here she paused for breath a moment, and I assured her that my thinking powers were equal to the feat. For, close to where I stood, there was a crack between the boards of fully half an inch in breadth; while by the window was another, through which I was able to thrust my closed umbrella, which is not so slim in figure as the present fashion goes.

Half of the shed contained a big four-poster bedstead, with the unusual addition of a mattress, sheets, and counterpane, and not the common substitute of some straw stuffed in a sack. The floor was further covered by an ancient chest of drawers, of loose and rickety appearance, as though they had been rather dissolute in youth. Clearly they had fallen into evil company, for of their handles some were missing, and I could see no pair that matched. There were small strips of muslin pinned as curtains to the window, which if opened, as was plain from the absence of a sash-line, it was difficult to shut. In the way of useful furniture, I saw three chairs with broken

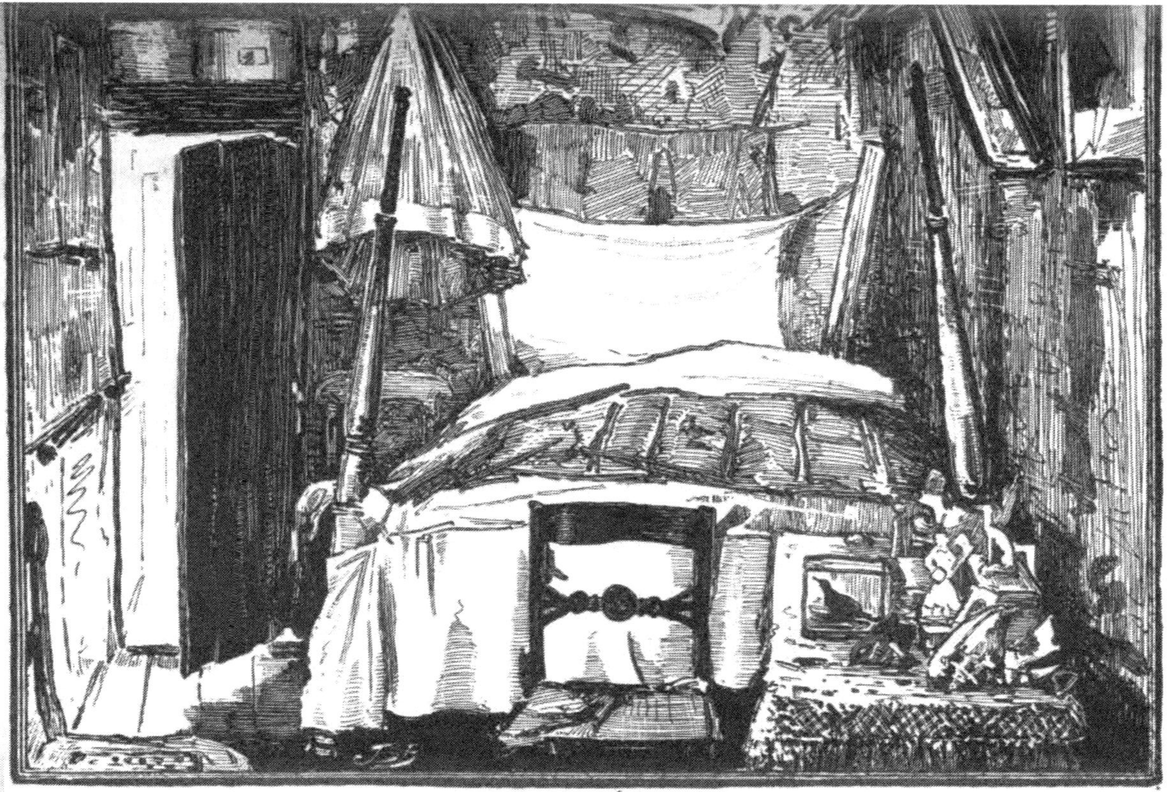

Face page 118.

backs; and two tables, which had likewise
been severely wounded, and were propped
against the wall. It seemed as though
they had retired from active service, and
were pensioned off for life. For fear it
might be moved, and come thereby to
sudden grief, one of the tables had
apparently been used as a museum or
asylum for old ornaments that had fallen
to decay. A lot of cracked or broken
shells, and several ugly knick-knacks, were
carefully arranged on it; together with a
tea-caddy which had seen better days, and
a starling that had apparently moulted just
ere it was stuffed. A row of brightly polished
tins made for common kitchen use, were
hanging by the fireplace, and formed a
useful contrast to the treasures on the table,
which seemed hardly worth the dusting
that their mistress must have given them
to make them look so clean. But doubtless
these poor relics were precious to their
owner, and possibly suggestive of some
family remembrance, or they would not
have been kept and tended with such care.

The polish of the tins deserved the highest
praise. They really seemed to brighten
the wretched, windy shed, and give it quite
a homely and habitable look. No wonder
their poor mistress took some pride in their
appearance, for she modestly avowed that
she had cleaned them all herself.

"We're poor enough," she added, "but
I can't abear no dirt, I can't. And no
more can't my son neither, though it's a
bit more in his line like, seein' as he lives
by it. He's a shoeblack, he is; an' if
boots didn't get dirty, why they'd never

want no cleanin', and that 'ud be a baddish job for him, and 'underds sech as he—them as has to get their livin' by the brush. Yes, they're mices 'oles they are, an' ratses 'oles as well too. We've plenty of 'em here we have. Don't want to go an' pay a shillin' for to see 'em at the Soho Logicals. Don't see 'em much by day, we don't, but they comes out pretty bold when it's a bit darkish. 'Pon my word they does, an' there, you 'ardly would believe it, but at night they squeal an' squeak so, it's for all the world like being at a con-sort. That's why we keeps that little dog there. If it worn't for him a barkin', they'd reglar eat us up a'most, when we're a sleepin'! Speshly my poor son, 'cause he've his bed upon the floor there—yes, sir, 'tis me sleeps in the bed, both me an' the young person as is a lodgin' here, you know."

This young person was out working, and bore a fair repute for industry and tidiness.

"She wouldn't be a living here else," said the woman somewhat sternly. "I can't abide no dirt, an' I can't abide no hidleness, an' where you finds the one, you mostly finds the hother. But she's a good girl is Mariar, an' she works 'ard to hearn a livin'. Nor she don't fling it away neither in finery an' fal-lala. And my boy, too, he's a good 'un, and he works 'ard too for his livin'. A rare good son is Tom, though he's baddish in the 'ead a' times. Tries all'ys to ack right, he do, though a bit wrong in his mind, poor chap. I were laid up wi' the fever, an' I weaned him on cold water, 'cause times were baddish, then, an' we couldn't buy no milk for him.

"That little dog there."

"I can't abide no dirt I can't."

Face page 120.

Mebbe that's what's made him weak like.
But I dunno as it's 'armed 'im. Half a
hidiot, some calls him, but he's more nor
half a good 'un. He's a Teetottler, is my
Tom, an' never done no 'arm to nobody.
An' he works 'ard for his livin' an' helps his
mother too, an' never takes no drink, an'
goes to gospel reg'lar, an' all the neighbours likes him an' respects him too, they
does; from a child to a queen's son they're
all'ys glad to see him, an' 'tain't a many
boys with more brains than my Tom, as
can say as much as that, you know."

It was little wonder that the poor widow
grew voluble when having for her subject
the virtues of her son, who, she said,
pursued his calling in the streets hard-by,
and would be twenty-five when his next
birthday came. Her mention of a queen's
son was of course a figure of speech, and
intended to convey a notion of high excellence. But if any royal scion were placed
beside her Tom, the one who would attain
the higher favour in her eyes certainly
would be the boy of lower birth.

Being questioned as to other members
of her family, she owned that she had had
six children, but now five of them were
dead, having been outlived by the weak-
ling, her first-born, of whose goodness the
poor mother appeared so justly proud.
Dull-witted as he was, the clear light of
Christ's teaching had peered into his mind.

"He seems to understan' it much better
nor I do," she explained, a little smiling, as
though at her own ignorance, and the
wisdom of her son. "And he ack up to
it a deal more," she continued to remark.

"There ain't a better Christian in all England, that there ain't. Not among the poor, nor yet among the rich, there ain't any man alive as try to do his duty better'n my poor boy. But he've reg'lar got religion in him, that's where it is, you know. Seems a'most to have been born in 'im, for he've never larned his letters. Ah, it's a rare thing is religion, 'speshly with the poor it is."

This she said without a smile, although there was a shade of irony, perhaps, in the assertion—taken literally, at least, and according to the common meaning of the words. Commenting on a text that hung beside the bed, she added: "'As one whom his mother comforteth.' Ah, that's often brought me comfort like, when I've been cryin' about my children. I couldn't comfort of 'em much, poor souls, while they was a living. But I make no doubt they're all in comfort now they're dead."

She answered heartily, "God bless you!" when we said good-bye to her, and she even caught my hand and kissed it, I confess to my surprise. I had given her no alms, nor was known to her in any way, nor had I promised any help in the dark days that might come to this poor dweller in a shed. Perhaps her mother's heart was touched by the thought of her lost children; and possibly she felt in need of some new outlet for her tenderness and love.

TRAVELS IN THE EAST.

PART VIII.*

"WHAT I want is, Facts!" cried the worthy and enlightened Mr. Gradgrind, in Hard Times.

I hope that I can claim no close resemblance to that gentleman; but I own it was a want precisely similar to his, which led me first to start upon my Eastern travels. I wished to see with my own eyes some of the homes of the poor workers, who are living there remote from the fine folk of the West. I wanted to inspect the actual condition of these much-talked-of abodes, and see if they were overcrowded, or falling to decay; and if any of the dwellers were half stifled or half starved. I wished to gain some knowledge of the ways and means of living of these poor working-people; and to hear from their own lips what complaints they had to make about their labour and their life.

If the reader chance to share my appetite for facts, he may thoroughly rely on the reality of those which I have introduced. Devourers of light literature may find diet of this sort too substantial for their taste; and I have tried therefore to mix a little

* ALL THE YEAR ROUND, April 19, 1884.

fancy with my facts, by way of flavouring the dish. But my fancies have been based on solid fact; as a good deal of light cookery is founded upon flesh. Some of the facts I have had to handle were unpalatably dry; and some not wholly savoury; and some, perhaps, a trifle coarse. Indeed, there seemed but little hope of their being at all relished, unless they could be served with just an appetising sprinkle—I dare not say, of Attic salt, but I may, perhaps, describe it as some literary sauce.

The scenes I have tried to picture have been really faithful drawings, done in pen and ink, and enlarged from the rough sketches I had pencilled on the spot. I have not wished to paint things blacker than they looked, nor have I clapped on lots of colour to heighten the effect.

But the reader must remember, while he joins me in my travels, that the dwellings I describe are not the dens where thieves live, or the haunts of wretched vice. Slums they may be, some of them, and foul, and ill-built, and ill-cleansed, and crowded overmuch for either decency or health, and going rapidly to ruin for mere want of due repair. Still, they are the so-called decent dwellings of the hard-worked honest poor, who have the happiness to live in this free and happy land.

A Royal Commission is now sitting on the subject, and collecting evidence from witnesses, presumably most competent to give it, and to aid with their experience towards amendment of the evils which undoubtedly exist. Whether or not these noble people may really lend a helping hand in better housing of King Mob, is more than can be prophesied. Let us hope that they may at any rate assist in the not distant dethronement of King Job, who has far too long reigned paramount in many a vestry parliament, and swayed his baleful sceptre over many a Poor Law Board.

Having thus relieved my mind, I may proceed with a light step upon my last travels in the East.

The sun was brightly shining when I met my guide at noon; and in the gardens of the West I left the lilacs large in bud, and the pear-trees near to bloom. The elms and chestnuts here and there were actually green; and in their boughs the birds were twittering. Here in the East, however, such spring's delights as these were not to be discerned. Hardly a tree was visible; and scarce even a sparrow, while basking in the sunshine, was blithe enough to chirp. Indeed, the sunshine seemed to deepen the shadows of the scenery, to search out its defects, and to show them up in prominence with a shaming, scorching light.

The ways by which we went through the wilds of brick and mortar were similar to those which we had previously traversed. There was little to relieve their dreary, dull monotony. All the streets were straight and narrow; some indeed so narrow that two carts could hardly pass. All were thronged with ragged children, making believe to play, and having rarely

anything to play with, except perhaps a
sickly baby, or a broken hoop. All were
bounded on each side by a dingy, low-
roofed row of dirty yellow houses, with
not one single inch of ornament, and conspicuously mean in their cheap and ugly
make. There were few shops to be seen,
and these made no outward show; and
even the small beer shops, which seemed
to be abundant, had few loungers at their
doors.

The children seemed to have the streets
all to themselves, for scarce a man was to
be met, and only here and there a woman,
either carrying a baby, or else hurrying
along as though hastening to her work.
Here and there a cat was crouching in a
doorway, or creeping along furtively in
quest of some stray food. Now and then
a cock gave a melancholy crow, and was
answered in the distance by a still more
dismal rival. The shrill whistle of a railway resounded now and then; but that is
not the kind of whistle which betokens a
light heart.

While on our way through this sad
wilderness we had some chat with one of
the few men whom we met. He was
standing in his doorway, which his large
figure well-nigh filled, and he returned
with interest the greeting of my guide, in
whom he seemed to recognise a friend in
case of urgent need. A group of tiny,
ragged, dirty little children were gathered
near the gutter, and were performing a
small war-dance round two babies who
seemed twins, and who were sitting bolt
upright, and with eyes wide open, in a

"Down there by the Blood 'Oles"

"As numerous as flies"

Face page 12

broken-down perambulator wherein they
were close packed. "They're as numerous
as flies," the man solemnly remarked; and
indeed the simile was not an ill-chosen
one; for the cluster of small creatures
seemed perpetually in motion, and making
an incessant disturbance for no adequate
result. I counted five - and - twenty in
a space of six yards square, and there
were other groups and scattered units
in the passage, for it was not quite a
street.

This man said that he had been living
"there or thereabouts for nigh on thirty
year," and had rarely found life harder
than he was doing now. Yes, he
worked down at the docks, he did, and
he'd most all'ys had been workin' there
since he came 'ome from furrin parts.
But three days out o' five there weren't
no work as he could get, and they didn't
seem to keer about keepin' their old 'ands
neither. And fresh comers they flocked in
so, why you was forced a'most to fight for
every bit of a job you get.

As he appeared an old inhabitant
I enquired whether he noticed any im-
provement in the neighbourhood in the
time during which he had been living
in it.

"Well, yes," he answered gravely, after
much inward meditation. "'Taint so bad
now as it were. Leastways, the outside of
it. This 'ere place weren't safe to henter
scarcely; leastways, arter nightfall, when
as I fust came to live 'ere. An' nobody
dustn't go much, not even by daylight,
mind you, down there by the Blood 'Oles."

The Blood Holes! A rare name this, methought, for a death-scene in a melo-drama. And the deep voice of the man seemed to make it sound more murderous. Still, we passed in safety through the sanguinary outlet from the passage where we left him, and by way of pleasant contrast, so far at least as the name went, we soon entered a Place which bore the title of Victoria, though there was little in its aspect to denote a royal residence.

There was a big dust-bin on the right hand of the place, put by way of useful ornament to decorate the entrance. Although not above half full (it being early in the week, that fine Monday afternoon), the dust-heap signified its presence quite as plainly to the nose, as by the eyes it was perceptible. That the dwellers in the court were not very exact marksmen in the shooting of their rubbish, and cared little for its presence, was patent from the way in which a peck or two of it lay scattered on the pavement, and added to the perfume of the ornamental reservoir.

The place contained ten houses, five on either side, and each of one small storey. Every house contained four rooms, and every room was probably the home of a whole family. With an average of less than four to each abode—or apartment if you please—the number of dwellers in the court, which was some twenty yards in length, would exceed one hundred and fifty. How often the dust-bin, that was common to them all, was cleaned out in the week, appeared a point which should be seen to, especially in summer, by the sanitary inspector.

The home which we there entered was the smallest I had seen, and, except perhaps the dustman's, it was certainly the dirtiest. Roughly guessed, its measurement was about eight feet by six, and not more than seven in height, and there was hardly a clean square inch in either floor, or walls, or ceiling. "Some walls won't take no paint," explained the mistress of the mansion, a plain, unwashed young woman, very slovenly in dress, and wearing one eye closed, clearly not by nature. The walls had once been partly blue, but now were chiefly black and brown with the dirt that had encrusted them. They were, however, much concealed by a collection of cheap prints, some coloured and some plain, and, viewed as works of art, entirely without value. In their subject, some were sacred and many more were secular, and of these latter, some were sporting and others sentimental. I counted seventeen of these exquisite productions. The one which occupied the place of honour on the walls displayed a rather long and lacka-daisical young lady reclining on a sofa in a sadly languid posture while a bevy of small persons, with their hair neatly curled, but with very scanty clothing, were floating in a sort of rainbow overhead. This delightful scene was labelled "The Believer's Vision," and, its gilded frame included, could hardly have been purchased for less than eighteenpence.

The works of art excepted, there was

little in the room of either ornament or use, barring an old bedstead with a heap of huddled sacking, whereon was a lean kitten of rather a sad look. She seemed ashamed of being seen in a place of such untidiness, and was pursuing under difficulties the labour of a wash. Some cheap and dirty crockery was scattered on a shelf, and prominent on the mantelpiece was a group whose date of birth it was easy to determine at a leash of decades since. It showed the Queen in a red robe, with a gilt crown on her head, and a scarlet pair of cheeks. She was standing quite erect, between a dapper little Frenchman and a lesser fez-capped Turk. As a sign of her supremacy, she overtopped her brave allies by more than half a head in stature, this being in their measurement as much as half an inch.

"Me an' my 'usbin an' the child the three of us we sleeps in this 'ere little room," cried the young woman in a breath, and then added in another : " But we've a littler room be'ind you know which we 'ires it all hincluded in the three-an'-six a week."

Proceeding to this smaller room, we found her statement of its size to be literally true. It hardly could have measured more than five feet, say, by six. Two panes of glass were broken in the window, but still the tiny chamber had a close and stuffy smell. A limp and dirty pillow, and a little pile of sacking, lay crammed into a corner; and, except a broken chair, there was no other furniture to hide the filthy floor.

St Patrick's
Supporter

The last of seven

Face page 1:

"Mother an' the little girl sleeps here,"
continued she, and introduced us to the
lady, who looked vastly like her daughter,
in so far as both their faces sadly
needed soap. Mother was employed in
sewing a large sack. It measured five feet
long, and was meant to hold four bushels,
so the worker said. She had to sew both
sides, and to hem all round the top. The
pay was sixpence for thirteen of them, and
she could do "two turns," that was twice
thirteen, a day. Yes, it were stiffish work,
she owned, and it hurt your hands a bit,
leastways till they got 'ardened like. But
she was glad enough to get it, for work
was precious slack.

Mother further stated that her age
was "fifty-two, come August," and that
her daughter, with the closed eye, was the
only one alive out of her seven children,
and that the little girl who slept with her
was not one of her family, nor in any way
related to her. "Mother keeps 'er 'cos
she's a Norphun," explained the daughter
simply ; as though that were a sufficient
reason for the housing of the little stranger,
who, she said, was then at school.

While this dialogue proceeded, another
dirty-faced young woman, with her hair unkempt and tangled, entered the small room,
and her tongue soon began to wag as rapidly
as the daughter's, who seldom let her mother
have a chance of saying much. The new
comer brought a big sheet, which she had
begun to sew. As the work demanded
special attention to the stitches, no less
than twopence would be earned when it
was done. No, it wasn't a quick way

to make a fortune, she confessed; but
it was better than making hammocks.
Besides sewing fifty holes, you had to
stitch two double seams; and half-a-score
of hammocks only brought you four and
threepence, and you had to work hard to
do a score a week. Still, this was not so
bad as making labels for the post-bags; for
you got half-a-crown a hundred, and it
took you all your time to do a hundred in
a week. The matchbox trade, however, was
by general consent esteemed the worst of
all, and my young friend Little Mother was
considered very lucky to get as much as
threepence for filling fifty boxes, that being
more than double the current market
price.

Close outside the broken window, in a
desolate back yard, there stood a little
barefooted boy of four or five, wearing, to
mark his nationality—it was St. Patrick's
Day—a green bow at his breast. He had
blue eyes and brown hair, a ragged pair
of trousers, and a pinkish pair of cheeks.
Their roses had been washed, just washed,
in a shower, or in some soap-and-water,
which, if less poetical, perhaps had cleaned
them even better, and made him a marked
contrast to the ladies of the court.* As a
reason for his standing there, they explained that he was "playing," though
certainly the fact was not apparent from
his attitude, and he had nothing to play
with, and nobody to play with him.

Beckoned to approach, he entered very

---

* Perhaps it is worth mention that in all my
travels I only saw one hand-basin.

promptly, with a smile on his clean face, and being presented with a penny, and asked what he would do with it, he replied very promptly, "Give it to mother," and departed so to do.

Mother appearing shortly after, I enquired if Master Timothy had performed his promise, and she replied, " Yes, shure," and said he was a good boy, and never broke his word. She was cleanly in her dress, and grave in her demeanour; and indeed her gravity was not without good cause. Her husband had died suddenly when Tim was a year old, and she was left with seven children to bring up. " Shure, they're mostly livin' out now, and a doin' for theirselves, they are; and beside meself and Tim here, there's but three of 'em to slape upon the flure wid us upstairs now."

" Do you ever see a clergyman, or a district visitor ?" I enquired of the four women, who now were gathered round me, and who, though living in one house, were inhabitants, in fact, of three distinct abodes. I had more than once put the question in my travels, and had been invariably answered in the negative; whereat I had not greatly wondered, being mindful of the miles and miles of misery around me, and the amazing multitude of dwellings to be visited, and the utter incapacity of the Church as now existent to cope with such vast work. However, here at last the query elicited assent—at least from two of the quartette.

" My clergyman comes to visit me," said the wife with the closed eye; and she spoke a little proudly, and emphasised the pronoun as though she kept a special parson solely for her private use. "And he's a priest," she added smartly, as if to heighten her importance in having the exclusive advantage of his visits. But her mother, with a pinch of snuff, appeared to sniff at such presumption, and cried: "Sure, he'll come to any one of us ; but why should we be troublin' him, exceptin' when we're dead ?" Whereto the sheetmaker, by a nod, appeared to signify assent, and the grave widow said, "That's true enough," and seemed to look more grave.

At the close of this conversation we left these poor women with a murmur of apology for taking up their time, which, however, they protested we had not done in the least. The street through which we went, on our departure from the court, looked sadly foul by sunlight, though my guide said that at night it was really like a fair. There were still a few signs visible of its nocturnal aspect. Locomotive shops were ranged along the pavement, and the hoarse cries of their keepers to attract a passing customer resounded in the air. Many houses in the neighbourhood had lately been pulled down as being too bad to be lived in, and there were many others which might fitly share their fate.

Five minutes of fast walking—as fast, at least, as we could go without trampling on the children, who anywhere and everywhere sat, or sprawled, or scrambled, or scampered in our way—another couple of furlongs, say, brought us well within sight of some shipping, and we soon found ourselves at

the end of a canal. As I was travelling
in the East, I might have mistaken it for
the Canal of Suez, let us say, had not my
guide informed me it was named after the
Regent of imperishable fame. Near to
this, and near the river, which lay hidden
from our view by some acres of tall brick-
work and some forests of tall masts (bricks
and masts both helping to make up what
so often in my travels had been mentioned
as the Docks), here suddenly I found myself
in a somewhat famous thoroughfare, which,
by dwellers in the East is known simply as
"The 'Ighway," but to which the name of
Ratcliff is added as a prefix by strangers
in the West.

Sailors abounded here: some yellow-
faced, some black, and many brown and
sunburnt. Of course, where Jack Tars
do abound, their Jills are sure to con-
gregate, and so the crowded pavements
were full of fair pedestrians, having
nothing on their heads, and doubtless
not much in them, except vanity or
viciousness. Seen by daylight these fair
sirens appeared gifted with few charms
that could render them alluring. Nor
seemed there much attraction in the caves
to which at nightfall they commonly resort.
These were shabby-looking haunts, though
bearing signs of festive import, such as
The Jolly Tar, or The Jovial Sea
Captain. Jack's alive till midnight in
these vicious drink-and-dancing shops, and
if he filled his pockets ere he started on
the spree, he will empty them long ere
the cruise ashore is ended.

Not far from the Highway, and too close

to escape from its contaminating influence,
we discovered a small court, which, by
way of dismal augury, bore the dreary
name of Chancery. We further were informed that it lay near to Angel Gardens,
a name which very likely had been chosen
for a contrast. Here in a low room of less
than twelve feet square, whereof the staircase formed a part, we found three women,
a red baby, and a little sleeping girl. The
floor was bare and dirty, and the ceiling
nearly black. Both sadly needed mending,
as did likewise the window and the walls.
The eldest woman said the weekly rent
was now four shillings for the house, which
only held two rooms, and looked scarce
strongly built enough to hold so much as
that.

She was a widow with eight children,
of whom the sleeping girl was one. The
younger mother with the baby, who was
just a fortnight old, had given birth to
three, and the still younger woman, who
was stitching at a sack, looked likely
before long to increase the yearly rising
population of the court.

Near this dirty Court of Chancery, I
made my first appearance in a common
lodging-house. Really, by comparison, it
looked quite a cleanly, comfortable place.
"Everything as heart could wish for as
regards cleanliness, it is here," exclaimed,
with a proud emphasis, the grey-bearded
old guardian, who smacked somewhat of
the sea, and the strict discipline of ships.
He informed us that permission to slumber
in his paradise was granted upon payment
of fourpence for a night. There were

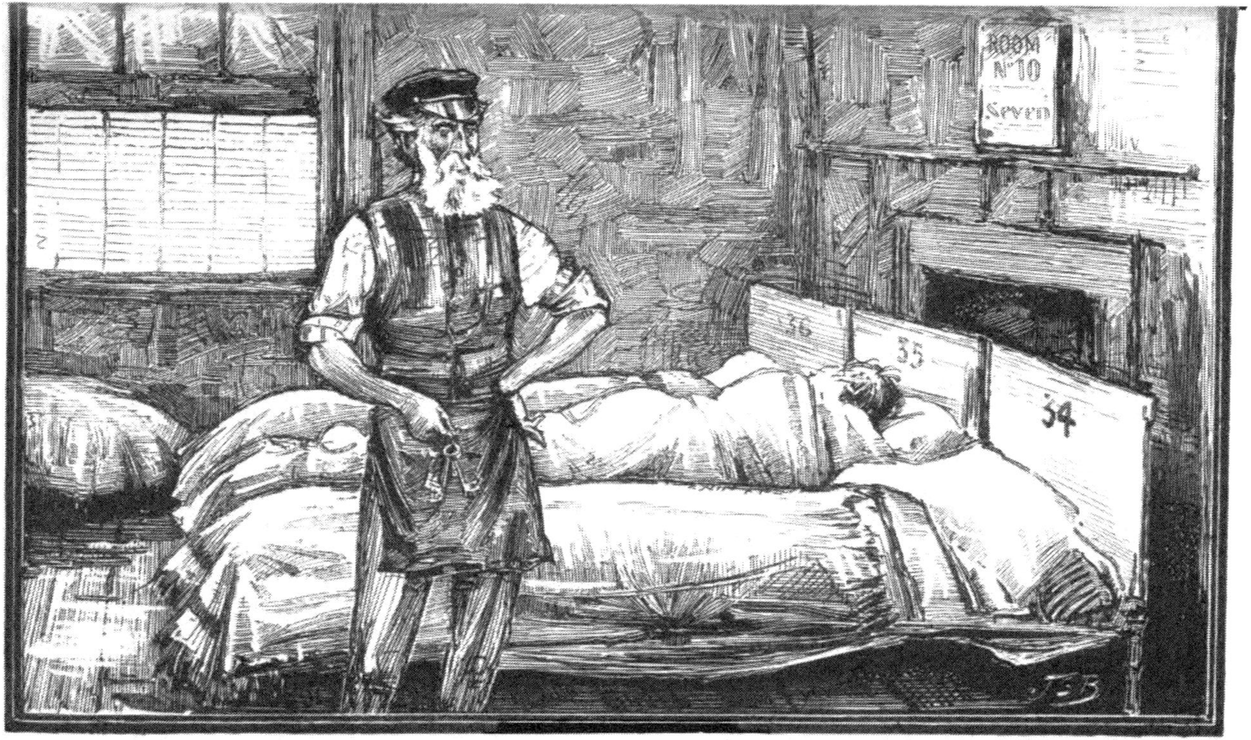
ROOM
Nº 10
Seven
36
35
34

"Four pence a night"

Face page 136.

about fifty beds within his care ; not very
long nor large they were, but "quite as
big as you could hope to get for fourpence,"
he remarked. Each had a brown coverlet,
and looked neat and tidy, and clearly the
bare floor had been most scrupulously
scrubbed. "You see, it's a compulsory
affair," he observed with a smile, and a
sharp staccato nod, which was as expres-
sive as a wink. "Police inspectuses us,
you know. Drops in of a sudden, and are
down on us like a shot. So if we've a
mind to be grubby, we must get our grub
elsewheer."

He smiles rather grimly as he makes his
little joke, and smiles with still more
grimness when I question him concerning
the habits of the gentlemen who come to
his hotel. "Ah, they're a queerish sort o'
customers. Queer characters they are, some
of them. Leastways, them as drop in
casual like. 'Cause we've a many as come
reg'lar, an' keep to their own beds. No,
they don't bring not much luggage. They've
just got the clothes they're wearing, and if
they've extry in a bundle, they pops 'em
down hunder the bolster. Nor they don't
hand me over many walables to keep for
'em. If so be they've got a gold watch,
or a set o' di'mond studs, as they're pertickler proud o' wearing, perhaps afore they
come they asks their Huncle to take keer
of 'em."

Briefly, with few details, I must sum-
marise my final six hours' journey in the
East. I saw a score of families in this
short space of time, and heard everywhere
the same complaining : of high rent for

wretched house-room, and of low wages
for hard work. Here I found a widow,
who contrived with an old mangle to earn
a scanty living for herself and her two
children ; one, a boy of eighteen, having
been born blind. There I came across a
labourer who had spent a fruitless morning
in waiting at the docks. "I was there at
half-past five," he said, "but there was no
job to be had. I hadn't nought for break-
fast but just a little bite o' bread ; an' if it
warn't for a bit o' baccy as I got from an
old friend, I should ha' fell down in a
faint." His face was pale, but cleanly
shaved ; and his boots were nicely blacked.
His wife, too, was as neat as her poor
means would suffer. They had four boys
to clothe, and two of them to feed, and all
four slept with them in one tiny little room.

Near them we found a costermonger,
who, unlike most of his trade, had a
clean, rosy pair of cheeks. He had been
selling mackerel since daylight, so he said,
and had been doing "pretty middling," he
candidly confessed. He was sitting at his
tea, having a score still to be sold ere he
ended his day's work. His wife had blessed
him with ten children, of whom the first
born was a soldier, on service now in
India, and the last born was a baby, who
was taking some refreshment from the
maternal breast. Seven of them slept,
together with their parents, in a couple of
small rooms, one hardly seven feet square.
The sleepers in the back room had their
beds, that is, their old sacks, laid upon
empty fish-boxes, as the ground was rather
damp.

Then we visited a widow, neat and
cleanly like her child, who "never saw his
father," she pityingly remarked. Her four
children all slept with her in one little bed,
which was as tidy as the room which made
their little home, and measured barely nine
feet long by not quite seven in breadth.
"I haven't had a bit of dinner, nor tea
neither, these two days," she replied to a
question; and added simply, "It feels
grievous to have the children, and not
know how to feed them;" this being said,
not in a begging way, but as stating a sad
fact.

We likewise spent ten minutes with the
wife of a dock labourer, who "drank dreadful" once, and then was "all'ys rowing"
her; but who, thanks to my guide's good
mission-work, had happily reformed. She
had had ten children, whereof the first
had died of "cholery," and only four were
now alive. The two big lads slept in
the small bed, "and the little 'uns in
t'other 'un with me and my good man."
He had hardly had a full day's work for
the last fortnight. Sometimes he'd get a
job "as would last him night and day,"
and then he would perforce "go two days
idle, and p'raps more. And that takes
the beauty off of it," she figuratively
remarked.

Also we went into a cellar, which, some
while since, was famous; a poor woman
who had lived there, having died of sheer
starvation, after bringing into life a
miserable babe. The place was ten feet
square, and exactly six feet in height. It
contained a biggish bed, wherein slept

father and mother, while Jane and Charley somehow lay crosswise at the foot. In a small bed by the window slept a big lad of fifteen; while the eldest girl, who owned that she was "going on for twenty," slumbered somehow in a corner, with a child of "not quite three," and a sister "turned sixteen."

In the back yard, which seemed common to the row of meagre tenements wherein this cellar had a place, I observed two little figures who recalled to me the pair of wretched, abject children who were introduced by the Ghost of Christmas Present to Mr. Scrooge by the names of "Ignorance" and "Want." Stunted and half starved, uncared for and unkempt; with one scanty bit of sackcloth to serve in lieu of clothing; with pale though filthy faces, and bare legs reddened with rough usage, and well-nigh black with dirt; they stared at me half savagely, and then scampered to some hiding-place like two small, scared, wild beasts. Poor wretched little creatures! Who could be their keeper? They were the saddest specimens of civilised existence I had met with in the East; and as I went upon my way—for I could find no entrance to the hole where they were hid—I reflected that the School Board would find fit work to do with pupils like to these. Moreover, I reflected that if living human creatures were constrained to stay in styes, it scarce needed Circe's art to turn them into brutes.

Last of all we visited a weakly, hollow-eyed, poor woman, who sat shivering by a fire, with a lean baby in her lap. She had six other children, one of whom was

Face *page* 141.

dumb, and was sitting opposite. Rheumatic-fever had prostrated her for several months, she said; and, but for my guide's help, she thought she must have died. Her husband, a dock labourer, had been near dying too. "It was the wet clothes, and waiting in the damp, as floored him," she opined. Well, yes, she would own that he had once been given to drink a bit; but "he's reg'lar cured of that," she said with a wan smile, and a flutter of her faint voice. He had long since signed the pledge, and had never once relapsed into his old vice, thanks mainly to my guide and the mission-folk who worked with him. "He's a different man now," the poor woman continued, "and I'm thankful, that I am, to them as made him give up drink."

And now I bid farewell to the poor people of the East, among whom I have recently been travelling a little, and with whom I have certainly been talking not a little, when I found them so inclined. If any word of mine may serve to help them in their ways, or in their work, or in their want, my travel and my travail will not have been in vain. Of my guide I will say simply, that his presence was welcomed wherever we walked, and that I thoroughly believe he is doing much good work.

THE END.

CHARLES DICKENS AND EVANS, GREAT NEW STREET, E.C.

LONDON COTTAGE MISSION

Instituted in the year 1870.

Offices: 44, FINSBURY PAVEMENT, LONDON, E.C.

This Society is supported by Voluntary Contributions, and is established for the Religious, Intellectual, and Social Elevation of the Working Classes, by means of Gospel Services held in Mission Halls, &c., Cottage Meetings held in the homes of the poor or otherwise, Addresses to Tramps and others in Lodging-house Kitchens, Open Air Preaching, Special Services for Children, Sunday Schools, Mothers' Meetings, Maternity Societies, Clothing and other Clubs, Bible Classes, House to House Visitation, Tract Distribution, Lectures on Self-help, Thrift, &c., and other Social and Religious Subjects, Entertainments and Concerts, Temperance Societies, Bands of Hope, and Excursions into the Country; also

For the Benevolent and Charitable purpose of Relieving the Sick and Destitute Poor by means of Temporary or Permanent Pecuniary Aid in deserving cases, weekly Irish Stew Dinners to poor Children, and gratuitous Distribution of Food, Fuel, and Clothing.

Also supports a large Convalescent and Country Home for poor Children, with nearly One Hundred Beds, at Halls Green Farm, Sevenoaks Weald, Kent.

FUNDS ARE URGENTLY NEEDED

To develop the good work the Mission has in view. Subscriptions and Donations will be gratefully received and acknowledged by Miss F. NAPTON, the Lady Superintendent, 304, Burdett Road, Limehouse, E.; the Bankers, THE LONDON AND SOUTH-WESTERN BANK, 7, Fenchurch Street, E.C.; and by WALTER AUSTIN, *Managing Director*, 44, Finsbury Pavement, London, E.C.

FORM OF BEQUEST.

I give unto the LONDON COTTAGE MISSION *in London, the Sum of   Pounds sterling, to be paid out of that part of my personal estate which by law may be effectually given for the benefit of the said Mission, and for which sum the receipt of the Treasurer for the time being shall be a sufficient discharge.*

Bankers:

THE LONDON & SOUTH-WESTERN BANK,

7, Fenchurch Street, London, E.C.

CPSIA information can be obtained
at www.ICGtesting.com
Printed in the USA
BVHW062357150919
558489BV00014B/1788/P

9 781166 592400